Cambridge IGCSE™
English as a Second Language

PRACTICE TESTS WITHOUT ANSWERS

Tom Bradbury, Mark Fountain & Melissa Thomson

Series editors: Katia Carter & Tim Carter

Shaftesbury Road, Cambridge CB2 8EA, United Kingdom

One Liberty Plaza, 20th Floor, New York, NY 10006, USA

477 Williamstown Road, Port Melbourne, VIC 3207, Australia

314–321, 3rd Floor, Plot 3, Splendor Forum, Jasola District Centre,
New Delhi – 110025, India

103 Penang Road, #05–06/07, Visioncrest Commercial, Singapore 23846

Cambridge University Press is part of the University of Cambridge.

It furthers the University's mission by disseminating knowledge in the pursuit of education, learning and research at the highest international levels of excellence.

www.cambridge.org
Information on this title: www.cambridge.org/9781009166089

© Cambridge University Press & Assessment 2023

This publication is in copyright. Subject to statutory exception and to the provisions of relevant collective licensing agreements, no reproduction of any part may take place without the written permission of Cambridge University Press & Assessment.

First published 2018
Second edition 2023

20 19 18 17 16 15 14 13 12 11 10 9 8 7 6 5

Printed in the Netherlands by Wilco BV

A catalogue record for this publication is available from the British Library

ISBN 978-1-009-16596-9 Paperback with digital access (with answers)
ISBN 978-1-009-16608-9 Paperback with digital access (without answers)

Cambridge University Press has no responsibility for the persistence or accuracy of URLs for external or third-party internet websites referred to in this publication, and does not guarantee that any content on such websites is, or will remain, accurate or appropriate.
....

NOTICE TO TEACHERS IN THE UK
It is illegal to reproduce any part of this work in material form (including photocopying and electronic storage) except under the following circumstances:
(i)   where you are abiding by a licence granted to your school or institution by the Copyright Licensing Agency;
(ii) where no such licence exists, or where you wish to exceed the terms of a licence, and you have gained the written permission of Cambridge University Press;
(iii) where you are allowed to reproduce without permission under the provisions of Chapter 3 of the Copyright, Designs and Patents Act 1988, which covers, for example, the reproduction of short passages within certain types of educational anthology and reproduction for the purposes of setting examination questions.

This resource has not been through the Cambridge International endorsement process.

The practice tests and mark schemes included in this resource have been written by the authors and provide students with an opportunity for additional practice. Questions in this resource will not appear in examinations. In examinations the way marks are awarded may be different. Any references to assessment and/or assessment preparation are the publisher's interpretation of the syllabus requirements.

While the publishers have made every attempt to ensure that advice on the qualification and its assessment is accurate, the official syllabus, specimen assessment materials and any associated assessment guidance materials produced by the awarding body are the only authoritative source of information and should always be referred to for definitive guidance.

CAMBRIDGE DEDICATED TEACHER AWARDS 2022

Teachers play an important part in shaping futures. Our Dedicated Teacher Awards recognise the hard work that teachers put in every day.

Thank you to everyone who nominated this year; we have been inspired and moved by all of your stories. Well done to all of our nominees for your dedication to learning and for inspiring the next generation of thinkers, leaders and innovators.

Congratulations to our incredible winners!

WINNER
Regional Winner
Australia, New Zealand & South-East Asia
Mohd Al Khalifa Bin Mohd Affnan
Keningau Vocational College, Malaysia

Regional Winner
Europe
Dr. Mary Shiny Ponparambil Paul
Little Flower English School, Italy

Regional Winner
North & South America
Noemi Falcon
Zora Neale Hurston Elementary School, United States

Regional Winner
Central & Southern Africa
Temitope Adewuyi
Fountain Heights Secondary School, Nigeria

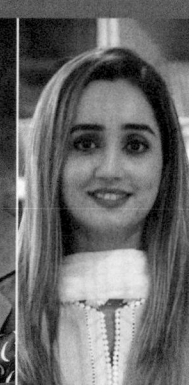
Regional Winner
Middle East & North Africa
Uroosa Imran
Beaconhouse School System KG-1 branch, Pakistan

Regional Winner
East & South Asia
Jeenath Akther
Chittagong Grammar School, Bangladesh

For more information about our dedicated teachers and their stories, go to
dedicatedteacher.cambridge.org

CAMBRIDGE UNIVERSITY PRESS

Brighter Thinking
Better Learning
Building Brighter Futures Together

Contents

Cambridge IGCSE™ English as a Second Language – introduction to the assessment	5
Assessment overview	6
Assessment objectives	9
Assessment criteria for Writing and Speaking	9
Marking students' work	14
Tick sheets (self-assessment for students)	17
Advice for students	19
Practice Test 1	21
Reading and Writing	21
Listening	35
Speaking	49
Practice Test 2	53
Reading and Writing	53
Listening	67
Speaking	81
Practice Test 3	85
Reading and Writing	85
Listening	99
Speaking	113
Practice Test 4	117
Reading and Writing	117
Listening	131
Speaking	145
Acknowledgements	149
Answer key (only included in the English as a Second Language practice tests with answers edition)	151

The digital resource contains:

    Audioscripts

    Additional speaking tests

    Example multiple-choice answer sheet

Cambridge IGCSE™ English as a Second Language – introduction to the assessment

The components of the Cambridge IGCSE™ English as a Second Language assessment are for speakers whose first language is not English. The assessment is mainly for students who are between 14 and 16 years old. It is recommended that students have completed approximately 130 guided learning hours before entering for the exams. However, the number of hours may vary depending on the previous experience of each student at the start of the course.

The expected level of language proficiency for students to cope well with the demands of the assessment is B2 on the Common European Framework of Reference.

There are four syllabuses: 0510, 0511, 0991 and 0993. The content of these syllabuses is identical. However, students who are entered for the 0510 and 0993 syllabuses (Speaking endorsement) are given a separate grade for their performance in the speaking component. Students who are entered for the 0511 and 0991 syllabuses (Count-in speaking) are given one grade for all three components: reading and writing, listening and speaking.

For syllabuses 0510 and 0511, grades A*– G are available with A* being the top grade and G being the lowest grade. For syllabuses 0991 and 0993 grades 9–1 are available with 9 being the top grade and 1 being the lowest.

Syllabuses 0510 and 0993 (Speaking endorsement)

Reading and Writing component:	Listening component:	Speaking component:
counts towards 70% of the final grade	counts towards 30% of the final grade	a separate grade is given

Syllabuses 0511 and 0991 (Count-in speaking)

Reading and Writing component:	Listening component:	Speaking component:
counts towards 50% of the final grade	counts towards 25% of the final grade	counts towards 25% of the final grade

Assessment overview

Disclaimer: The information in this section is based on the Cambridge International syllabus. You should always refer to the appropriate syllabus document for the year of examination to confirm the details and for more information. The syllabus document is available on the Cambridge International website at www.cambridgeinternational.org.

Reading and Writing paper*			
(2 hours)			
Exercises	**Assessment objectives tested**	**Tasks**	**Number of marks available (60 marks)**
Exercise 1	R1, R2, R3	Reading comprehension for specific detail	8 marks
Exercise 2	R1, R2, R3, R4	Multiple matching	9 marks
Exercise 3	R1, R2, R3	Note making	7 marks
Exercise 4	R1, R2, R3, R4	Multiple choice	6 marks
Exercise 5	W1, W2, W3, W4	Extended writing (informal email)	15 marks
Exercise 6	W1, W2, W3, W4	Discursive writing (formal/semi-formal article, report, essay or review)	15 marks

* Students are not allowed to use dictionaries.

Listening paper**			
(approximately 50 minutes, including the transfer time of 6 minutes)			
Exercises	**Assessment objectives tested**	**Tasks**	**Number of marks available (40 marks)**
Exercise 1 (Questions 1–8)	L1, L2, L3	Multiple choice with four visual options (includes monologues and dialogues)	8 marks
Exercise 2 (Questions 9–18)	L1, L2, L3, L4	Multiple choice, short extracts (includes dialogues and monologues)	10 marks
Exercise 3 (Questions 19–26)	L1, L2, L3	Multiple choice, sentence completion (a monologue)	8 marks
Exercise 4 (Questions 27–32)	L1, L2, L3, L4	Multiple matching (short monologues)	6 marks
Exercise 5 (Questions 33–40)	L1, L2, L3, L4	Multiple choice (interview)	8 marks

** Each part of the listening paper is played twice. At the end of the test, students are given 6 minutes to transfer their answers onto a separate answer sheet.

Speaking paper***				
(approximately 10–15 minutes)				
Parts	Duration	Assessment objectives tested	What happens	Number of marks available (40 marks in total for all three assessed parts)
Introduction	1 minute	N/A	The examiner welcomes the student and explains the procedure.	Not assessed
Warm-up	1–2 minutes	N/A	The examiner asks the student a few questions about their life and interests to put them at ease. For example: *What do you enjoy doing in your free time?*, *What are your favourite hobbies, and why?*, *What are your plans for the weekend?*, etc. This part is not assessed.	Not assessed
Part 1 – Interview	2–3 minutes	S1, S2, S3, S4	The examiner asks the student three questions on the same topic (e.g. *future career*). The examiner may ask extra questions such as *Can you tell me more about …?* to help the student develop their answers. The student can ask for clarification if necessary. This part is assessed.	Assessed
Part 2 – Short talk	3–4 minutes (including 1 minute for preparation)	S1, S2, S3, S4	The examiner gives the student a topic card with two ideas (e.g. *learning a new language, learning to cook*) and asks them to talk about, for example, the benefits and challenges of each idea. The student is given one minute to think about what they want to say. The student then delivers a short talk comparing and contrasting the two ideas on the topic card. At the end, the student should say which idea they would prefer and explain why. This part is assessed.	Assessed

Speaking paper*				
(approximately 10–15 minutes)				
Parts	**Duration**	**Assessment objectives tested**	**What happens**	**Number of marks available** (40 marks in total for all three assessed parts)
Part 3 – Discussion	3–4 minutes	S1, S2, S3, S4	The examiner asks the student questions (e.g. *Do you think learning online is easier than learning in the classroom?*) to further develop the topic used in part 2. The student discusses their ideas with the examiner. The examiner may ask further questions such as *Why do you think this is?* to encourage the student to develop their ideas and opinions. This part is assessed.	Assessed

*** The whole of the speaking test is recorded including the preparation part. The students are examined individually, **not** in pairs. The examiner and the student must speak in English throughout the whole test. Students are not allowed to write anything down or use dictionaries.

Assessment objectives

Disclaimer: The information in this section is based on the Cambridge International syllabus. You should always refer to the appropriate syllabus document for the year of examination to confirm the details and for more information. The syllabus document is available on the Cambridge International website at www.cambridgeinternational.org.

In the Reading exercises, you will be tested on your ability to:

1. Understand a specific piece of information
2. Understand how different ideas are connected (e.g. preference, agreement)
3. Find pieces of information by using the right reading strategy (e.g. scanning)
4. Understand ideas that are implied

In the Writing exercises, you will be tested on your ability to:

1. Express facts and opinions clearly
2. Group and link ideas clearly and produce a well-organised text
3. Use a range of words, phrases and grammatical structures
4. Use register (e.g. semi-formal) and style (e.g. a persuasive review, an informative report) appropriate for the given situation

In the Listening exercises, you will be tested on your ability to:

1. Understand factual information (e.g. names, times, places)
2. Understand more complex ideas (e.g. speakers' opinions, preferences, decisions)
3. Understand how different ideas are connected (e.g. agreement and disagreement)
4. Understand what speakers imply

In the Speaking exercises, you will be tested on your ability to:

1. Express ideas and opinions on a given topic
2. Use a range of words, phrases and grammatical structures
3. Produce well-developed answers and maintain a conversation
4. Pronounce clearly and use intonation to enhance what is being said

Assessment criteria for Writing and Speaking

The following criteria are designed to help with marking written and oral work. We have simplified the marking criteria used by Cambridge Assessment International Education in the Cambridge IGCSE English as a Second Language assessment so that they are accessible for students to understand success criteria.

If you wish to see the official marking criteria for Cambridge IGCSE English as a Second Language, please visit the Cambridge Assessment International Education website: **www.cambridgeinternational.org**.

Writing (Exercises 5 and 6)

Give a separate marks for content and language. The total number of marks available for each exercise is 15.

First, decide which band is the best fit for each category. If all, or most, of the criteria of the band are met, give the higher mark; if the answer only meets some of the criteria, give the lower mark. The content and language marks can be very different if necessary.

Marking the content:

- Award a maximum of 6 marks.
- Focus on task fulfilment, relevance and development of ideas and how long or short the answer is.
- If the answer is very short, only award 1–2 marks.
- If the answer contains some irrelevant material, only award 1–2 marks.
- If the answer has no relevance to the task, award 0 marks.

Marking the language:

- Award a maximum of 9 marks.
- Focus on the range of the grammatical structures and vocabulary used, the number and the type of errors that appear in the answer. Also focus on the organisation of ideas and how well they are linked together.
- Answers that contain partially irrelevant information, and receive 1–2 marks for content, can still be given up to 9 marks for language.
- Answers that have no relevance to the task, and receive 0 marks for content, should also be given 0 marks for language.

Content	
Description	**Marks**
The answer: • addresses the task completely • only includes content which is relevant to the task • uses an appropriate format and register throughout • shows an excellent understanding of purpose and audience • is very well developed • meets the word count requirement.	5–6
The answer: • mainly addresses the task • mainly includes content that is relevant to the task • uses mainly appropriate format and register • shows a good understanding of purpose and audience • is mainly well developed • meets the word count requirement.	3–4
The answer: • partially addresses the task • includes some content that is not relevant to the task • produces text with an inconsistent or inappropriate format and register • shows a lack of understanding of purpose and audience • shows minimal development • is below the required word count.	1–2
No creditable content	0

Language	
Description	**Marks**
The answer: • uses a broad range of both common and uncommon vocabulary • uses a broad range of simple and complex structures • uses language which is almost always accurate; any errors are in less common vocabulary or complex structures, and do not affect the reader's comprehension • is organised effectively • uses a broad range of linking words and devices.	7–9
The answer: • uses a range of common vocabulary, with some examples of less common vocabulary • uses a broad range of simple structures, and tries to use some complex structures • uses language which is mainly accurate; errors are mostly in less common vocabulary or complex structures, and do not affect the reader's comprehension • is reasonably well organised • uses a range of a range of linking words and devices.	4–6
The answer: • uses only common vocabulary • uses only simple structures • uses language which is sometimes difficult to understand, due to errors in common vocabulary and simple structures • shows only a basic attempt at organisation • uses a small range of linking words and devices.	1–3
No creditable content	0

Speaking

When using the marking criteria below, consider the student's responses to all tasks in the practice test except for the warm-up. Select a mark from 0–10 for each of grammar, vocabulary, development and pronunciation, then combine them to give a total mark out of 40.

Marks	Grammar	Vocabulary	Development	Pronunciation
9–10	• Student uses a range of simple and complex structures. • Student makes minimal errors in both simple and complex structures. • The meaning is always clear.	• Student can talk about and express opinions on a range of facts and ideas. • Student uses a wide range of vocabulary. • Student can use some vocabulary with precision.	• Student always responds relevantly and develops their ideas. • Student needs no or very little support to maintain communication.	• Student's pronunciation is always clear. • Student often uses intonation effectively to communicate the intended meaning.
7–8	• Student uses a range of simple structures and attempts to use some complex structures. • Student makes minimal errors in simple structures, but more frequent errors in complex structures. • The meaning is always clear despite the errors.	• Student can talk about and express opinions on a range of facts and ideas. • Student uses a reasonable range of vocabulary. • Student uses vocabulary correctly.	• Student responds relevantly and develops most of their ideas. • Student needs occasional support to maintain communication.	• Student can be understood despite some pronunciation issues. • Student sometimes uses intonation effectively to communicate the intended meaning.
5–6	• Student uses a range of simple structures, but complex structures are rarely used. • Student makes some errors in the structures used. • The meaning may sometimes be ambiguous because of the errors.	• Student can talk about and express opinions on simple facts and ideas. • Student uses a range of vocabulary. • Student uses most vocabulary correctly.	• Student responds relevantly and develops some of their ideas. • Student needs frequent support to maintain communication.	• Student can mostly be understood, but some effort is needed because of pronunciation issues. • Student rarely uses intonation effectively to communicate the intended meaning.

Marks	Grammar	Vocabulary	Development	Pronunciation
3–4	• Student uses a very limited range of simple structures. • Student makes frequent errors. • The meaning is often ambiguous because of the errors.	• Student can only talk about and express opinions on basic facts. • Student uses a limited range of vocabulary.	• Student provides some irrelevant responses and rarely develops their ideas. • Student has difficulty maintaining communication despite frequent support.	• Student can rarely be understood, effort is needed because of pronunciation issues. • Student doesn't use intonation effectively to communicate the intended meaning.
1–2	• Student only uses isolated words or simple short phrases. • The meaning is ambiguous throughout.	• Student has difficulty talking about and expressing opinions on even the most basic facts. • Student only uses extremely limited and repetitive vocabulary.	• Student only provides very short isolated responses. • Student cannot maintain communication despite frequent support.	• Student has serious pronunciation issues, which lead to a breakdown in communication. • Student doesn't use any intonation patterns.
0	No answer given	No answer given	No answer given	No answer given

Disclaimer: Please note that these marking criteria have not been produced by Cambridge Assessment International Education. The descriptors are based on Cambridge International's descriptors but have been written by the authors of this resource. If you wish to see the official marking criteria for the writing and speaking components of Cambridge IGCSE English as a Second Language, please visit the Cambridge Assessment International Education website.

Marking students' work

	Reading and Writing paper	
Exercises	**Answers which gain marks:**	**Answers which may lose marks:**
Exercise 1	• short answers lifted from the original text • alternative answers which have the same meaning as the answer in the text.	• poorly spelt answers where the meaning is not clear.
Exercise 2	• clearly written letters.	• more than one answer per question • a letter written over the initial answer which makes it difficult to decipher.
Exercise 3	• ideas lifted from the text that are clearly different from one another • answers which may be paraphrased ideas from the text but which retain the same meaning as the original ideas from the text • ideas written under the correct heading on a separate line.	• ideas that are too similar in meaning (only 1 mark can be awarded for two similar ideas) • correct answers written under the wrong heading • paraphrased answers which change the meaning of the original idea from the text • answers that are so badly misspelled that the meaning is not clear.
Exercise 4	• the answer is clearly indicated by a tick in one of the boxes.	• more than one box has been ticked for the same question.
Exercise 5	• the email contains answers to all of the bullet points from the question • the information given in the email is well developed and relevant to the ideas from the bullet points • the answer is written in the correct style and appropriate informal register • the email is of the correct length which is stated in the question • all the information in the email is clearly organised into paragraphs • ideas and paragraphs are linked using appropriate linking words and phrases (e.g. conjunctions, relative pronouns, adverbial phrases) • there is a range of vocabulary (e.g. phrasal verbs – *get on with, set off*; fixed phrases – *I was in two minds*) and grammatical structures (e.g. *I've never done anything like it, I shouldn't have gone there*) appropriate for an email • the email contains minimal errors, which only appear in more complex language structures, but these errors do not make it difficult for the reader to understand the ideas.	• some of the points from the question are omitted • the ideas in the email aren't relevant to the bullet points from the question • answers to each bullet point are not well developed and very brief • the email uses the wrong tone and inappropriate register, which would have a negative effect on the reader • the email is very short • the email lacks paragraphs and the information is not well organised, which makes it very difficult for the reader to understand • the sentences are very short with no or very basic linking words • the range of vocabulary and grammatical structures is very limited (e.g. mostly the present tense and very common vocabulary are used) • the email contains a number of errors and this makes it difficult for the reader to understand the ideas (e.g. wrong tenses, wrong word forms, missing words, misspelling).

Reading and Writing paper		
Exercises	**Answers which gain marks:**	**Answers which may lose marks:**
Exercise 6	<ul><li>the answer deals with the topic from the question (e.g. a report about the school canteen and recommend what needs to be improved), the ideas are relevant and the reader would be fully informed</li><li>the answer contains well-developed ideas (the ideas come from the prompts in the question and/or from student's own examples) and provides examples, reasons, explanations, opinions, etc.</li><li>the answer is written in the correct style (i.e. article, report, review, essay) and uses the appropriate register (semi-formal to formal)</li><li>the answer is of the correct length that is stated in the question</li><li>ideas are clearly organised into paragraphs (e.g. introduction of the topic/task, further information/ideas, conclusion/summary/recommendation)</li><li>ideas and paragraphs are linked with appropriate linking words and other phrases (e.g. *however, for instance, last but not least, which, as far as I'm concerned, to begin with*)</li><li>the answer contains a range of vocabulary and grammatical structures appropriate for the style and register</li><li>the answer contains minimal errors which only appear in more complex language structures, but these errors do not make it difficult for the reader to understand the ideas.</li></ul>	<ul><li>ideas that are not relevant and the reader would not be fully informed</li><li>the answer only copies ideas from the prompts in the question, these ideas are brief and not developed; the whole answer contains no, or very little, extra information on the topic</li><li>the answer is written in the wrong style and register, and uses a tone which would have a negative effect on the reader</li><li>the answer is very short</li><li>the answer lacks paragraphs and the ideas are poorly organised, which makes it difficult for the reader to understand</li><li>ideas are written as very short sentences with no or very basic linking words</li><li>the range of vocabulary and grammatical structures is very limited and inappropriate for the style and register</li><li>the answer contains a number of errors and this makes it difficult for the reader to understand the ideas (e.g. wrong tenses, wrong word forms, missing words, misspelling).</li></ul>

Listening paper		
Exercises	Answers which gain marks:	Answers which may lose marks:
1–3 and 5	• the answer is clearly indicated by a tick in one of the boxes.	• answers where more than one box is ticked even if one of these answers is correct.
4	• clearly written letters.	• the same letter is used twice.

Speaking paper		
Parts	Answers which gain marks:	Answers which may lose marks:
Parts 1–3	• student can discuss facts and ideas on a range of topics • student can develop their answers without the help of the examiner • answers are well developed and include examples, personal anecdotes, explanations, ideas and opinions for and against, comparisons, speculations, predictions, etc. • answers are relevant • student uses a range of grammatical structures, including more complex structures (e.g. relative clauses, conditionals, continuous and perfect aspects in tenses) • student uses a wide range of vocabulary, including some precise topic related vocabulary (e.g. collocations – *blissfully unaware, irreparable damage*; appropriate phrasal verbs – *live up to, get through to*; precise adjectives and verbs – *enormous, negotiate*) • student has clear pronunciation and uses intonation to define the meaning of their ideas (e.g. contrastive stress to correct facts and ideas, rising and falling intonation when adding extra information) • answers contain minimal errors which only appear in more complex language structures, but these errors don't cause any misunderstanding.	• student is not able to discuss more complex ideas on a range of topics • answers are widely spaced and the student needs a lot of prompting from the examiner in order to maintain the conversation • answers tend to be brief • some answers are irrelevant • student uses a very limited range of vocabulary and grammatical structures and this has a negative effect on the listener • the pronunciation is unclear and there are no intonation patterns used and this has a negative effect on the listener • answers contain frequent errors and the communication often breaks down.

Tick sheets (self-assessment for students)

The following tick sheets will help you think about what is expected of you in the exam and to look more critically at your own performance.

Reading tests		
Have you done the following? Put a tick (✓) in the appropriate box. HAVE YOU...	**Yes**	**No**
done what the instructions told you to do (e.g. use each letter only once)?		
highlighted the correct answers in the text, in case you need to go back to them later?		
written the answer on the line/in the space provided, under the correct heading, etc.?		
copied the answer as it is written in the text?		
provided a clear answer (e.g. crossed out the wrong answer to make sure your final choice is clear)?		
checked your answers after you finished doing each exercise?		

Writing test		
Have you done the following? Put a tick (✓) in the appropriate box. HAVE YOU...	**Yes**	**No**
answered all the points from the question?		
used the correct style (i.e. email, report, review, article, essay) and register (i.e. informal, semi-formal)?		
developed your answers/ideas (e.g. given an example, explained the reason, agreed/disagreed with an idea)?		
used paragraphs?		
included a good beginning and ending to your piece of writing?		
used complex sentences, where appropriate, and linking words/phrases to link your ideas?		
used a range of vocabulary and grammatical structures?		
used a capital letter to start a new sentence and a full stop or a question mark to finish each sentence?		
spelt your words as correctly as possible?		
written a piece of writing of the right length?		
checked for mistakes at the end and corrected as many as you could (e.g. tenses, missing articles, wrong prepositions)?		

Listening test		
Have you done the following? Put a tick (✔) in the appropriate box. HAVE YOU…	Yes	No
done what the instructions told you to do (e.g. use each letter only once)?		
checked your answers after you finished listening to each exercise?		
transferred your answers onto a separate answer sheet at the end of the test?		

Speaking test		
Have you done the following? Put a tick (✔) in the appropriate box. HAVE YOU…	Yes	No
answered the examiner's questions as fully as possible?		
supported your ideas/opinions with examples from your own experience (e.g. personal anecdotes)?		
given reasons for your ideas/opinions?		
made some comparisons (e.g. you and your friends, at present and in the past)?		
speculated about the positive and negative points?		
explained your preference?		
agreed or disagreed with the ideas/opinions expressed in the questions?		
asked for clarification, if necessary?		
linked your ideas/opinions with appropriate linking words and phrases?		
used a range of grammatical structures (e.g. tenses, conditionals, relative clauses)?		
used a range of vocabulary (e.g. descriptive adjectives and verbs, phrasal verbs, fixed expressions)?		
made sure you sounded clear?		
thought about the correct way of saying things in English to reduce the number of errors you make?		

Advice for students

Before the exam

- familiarise yourself with the format of each part of the test
- learn about some useful exam techniques which will help you answer each part of the test more successfully
- do practice tests to see which parts you are good at and which parts you need to focus on more
- time yourself to see how much time you take to complete each part of the test
- look at your own mistakes and analyse them
- set yourself realistic targets.

During the exam

- try to relax
- when you open the exam paper, first look through the whole test quickly to see what you have to do
- set yourself a time limit for each part of the exam to make sure you have enough time to complete each part
- try to use all the exam techniques you learnt in your lessons
- read the rubrics for each exercise and follow the instructions given
- if you do not know an answer, guess – never leave any blank spaces
- if you change your answer, cross out the wrong answer to make it clear which answer is your final choice
- in the writing part of the exam, always spend a minute or two planning your answer first (e.g. what ideas to include, how many paragraphs, what information to include in each paragraph) before you start writing
- in the listening exam, remember to transfer your answers onto a separate answer sheet at the end of the test, you will be given 6 minutes to do that
- if you have enough time left, check your answers.

BLANK PAGE

Practice Test 1
Reading and Writing

Exercise 1

Read the article about a woman called Li Daniels, who is a chef, and then answer the questions.

LI DANIELS – COOKERY COMPETITION WINNER

Li Daniels grew up in the Malaysian city of Malacca, and when she moved to Liverpool in the UK to study economics ten years ago, she found things tough. Everything seemed so different, but the hardest thing to get used to was the food. 'I missed Malaysian food so much,' says Li. And she had no idea how to cook. Malaysians usually learn from their mothers, but Li's mother had always banned her from the kitchen. So, Li taught herself. It was hard at first, but she soon grew to love cooking.

Li is now married to Chris Daniels, a businessman, and they have a three-year-old son. The family's intention is to move to London in the next few months. 'It'd be more convenient for me,' says Li.

Besides cooking family meals, Li enjoys organising dinner parties for friends. About a year ago, someone suggested Li should try *The Big Taste*, a cookery competition on television. 'It was Gina, a colleague from the bank I'd recently joined,' says Li. 'I'd moved there from an insurance company. It's incredible how Gina's words have affected my life. I'm even opening my own cafe later this year.'

Li entered *The Big Taste* with 50 other hopefuls. She survived ten weeks of challenges, from creating a tasty packed lunch to preparing a five-course meal for a special celebration, before reaching the final. 'Cooking for a top hotel was my personal highlight,' says Li.

It was an emotional experience for Li. 'I was really excited at first, but when the final became a possibility, I got very nervous.' In the last round, however, she was calm and cooked a wonderful fish stew dish to win the contest. 'It was extraordinary,' said one of the judges.

Li won over viewers from the very first episode and her success brought her lots of attention. Soon after her win, a publisher invited her to write a cookery book, called *Cooking with Li*, that has just been published. Li was also asked to supply some well-known restaurants with recipes and she says that will happen by the end of the year.

Li bases her recipes on traditional Southeast Asian dishes, but she experiments with them. Her sister and a few friends help her with ideas, and her husband tastes every recipe she comes up with. 'His opinion's important to me,' she says.

Now, besides looking after her family and promoting her book, Li gives demonstrations at food festivals and in restaurants. She also hopes to start filming a documentary series about spices in the coming few months. '*The Big Taste* definitely changed my life,' says Li.

Question 1

How did Li learn to cook?

.... [1]

Question 2

Where was Li working when she entered the cookery competition?

.... [1]

Question 3

Which part of the competition did Li enjoy most?

.... [1]

Question 4

How did Li feel during the competition final?

.... [1]

Question 5

Who always tries and comments on Li's new dishes?

.... [1]

Question 6

What plans does Li have for the future? Give **three** details.

....

....

.... [3]

[Total: 8]

Exercise 2

Read extracts from a magazine article in which four people (**A–D**) talk about the night before an important day in their working lives. Then answer Question **7 (a)–(i)**.

THE NIGHT BEFORE A BIG DAY

A   Actor, Harry McNeil

Actors are always in the theatre the night before the first public performance of a play. We spend time running through our lines, but everyone involved in the production is there doing the final preparations for the next day. My mind plays tricks on me when the pressure is on. I've been acting for nearly 10 years, but I still get visions of myself in front of a big audience not being able to remember anything I'm supposed to say or do. Some actors find a space where they can be alone and rest, but that doesn't suit me. I get anxious if I'm not doing something. Acting is mentally and physically exhausting, so it helps to keep fit, but I also get through a considerable quantity of sandwiches and pizza – far more than is good for me. When I eventually get home, I usually experience very little difficulty in falling asleep.

B   Astronaut, Simone Katz

I will soon be on my third space mission. On both previous occasions, I carried out repairs to the Space Station and was only there for a few days. This time, however, I'll be there for three months, doing research, spacewalks and lots of everyday tasks. I'm currently going through a training programme to get my physical fitness and skills to the levels required. By the night before take-off, I'll have adopted all the eating, sleeping and exercise patterns that we have to follow in space. On that last night, I'll telephone my parents and sister to say goodbye. Judging by my previous experiences, the conversations are unlikely to be relaxed; everyone knows things can happen in space, however carefully you prepare. I will also try to ensure that I get a few valuable hours to myself. It's rarely available when you're with your crew in the Space Station.

C   Professional cyclist, Matthew Jones

In the races I take part in, we can cover 3000 kilometres in under three weeks and we have to be extremely well prepared. In the evening between two days' racing, I always have a large meal. Professional cyclists like me are usually very slim, but you'd be surprised how much we eat; the food gives us energy. In the meantime, my bike receives any necessary maintenance. Without my backup team, I wouldn't be able to compete. At some point, I chat to my wife and son online. I'm away from home so much and for me it's vital to have that regular contact with them. I go to bed at nine o'clock and I usually listen to some music to take my mind off the race. It's better for me to start the next stage feeling fresh than to worry about it overnight, and music helps me relax and sleep.

D Surgeon, Monica Alvarez

Although I've been a surgeon for over 15 years, I still often lie awake for much of the night before a big operation. This used to upset me, but I've come to see it as normal. Operations can be long and exhausting – I may do three or four in a day and twelve-hour working days are not uncommon – so in the evening before a major operation, I avoid doing anything very energetic. I sit down to a good dinner with my husband and children and we catch up on each others' days. My children don't always understand why I ask them about what they've been doing at school and with their friends, and what they're going to do tomorrow, but I want to know these things. I also spend an hour or so drawing. I use pencils and ink to do cartoons aimed at teenagers like my own children. I've been doing it for a few years now, and I find it restful and satisfying.

For each question, write the correct letter A, B, C or D on the line.

Question 7

Which person…

(a) accepts that they may not sleep well? .... [1]

(b) imagines how things could go wrong for them? .... [1]

(c) tries to avoid thinking about the following day? .... [1]

(d) feels the need to spend some time on their own? .... [1]

(e) prefers to stay busy? .... [1]

(f) explains what they rely on other people for? .... [1]

(g) thinks they eat too much? .... [1]

(h) benefits from taking part in a creative activity? .... [1]

(i) finds it difficult to talk to family members? .... [1]

[Total: 9]

Exercise 3

Read the article about a dinosaur expert called James Bruce, and then complete the notes.

THE DINOSAUR EXPERT

James Bruce is one of the world's leading palaeontologists. In other words, he is a dinosaur expert who studies fossils, the remains of animal bones that are millions of years old. James's interest was sparked at the age of 14 when he saw a dinosaur movie at the cinema. 'I loved the special effects and the idea that such amazing animals had been on earth millions of years ago,' he says. 'Then I got obsessed with theories of what caused the dinosaurs to disappear. That still fascinates me and I wish I had time to study it now.' Twenty-five years after that cinema trip, James teaches palaeontology at a university and travels around the world looking for dinosaur fossils.

James's experience as a teenager is one reason why he is now unwilling to criticise dinosaur movies for being scientifically inaccurate. He understands that they are meant to entertain, and the fact that the dinosaurs in them move much faster than was actually the case 100 million years ago doesn't concern him. 'The ones you see in films are also a lot more intelligent than they could possibly have been,' he says. 'But if the films get people interested in dinosaurs by telling a good story, that's a good thing.'

James has spent some of the last three years advising makers of TV documentaries on the subject of dinosaurs. He checks that the animals reconstructed for the documentaries are as close as possible to what scientists know about dinosaurs. 'We have a good idea from fossils what sizes different species were. The ones you see in movies are often bigger than the evidence indicates. And in movies, dinosaurs are shown as darker and less colourful than they were in reality,' he says. 'That's to make them look scary.'

However, James admits there's much that is still unknown about dinosaurs. 'We have very little idea about how they interacted with each other – you can't work it out just from studying bones,' he says. Also, there are various theories about what sounds dinosaurs might have made, but the evidence is limited. 'I'm very keen to investigate both of those issues,' James says.

One project he worked on was part of a wider international programme, which established that modern-day birds are directly related to dinosaurs. It was this discovery that led James and other palaeontologists to conclude that many species of dinosaur were covered with feathers. 'All the dinosaurs we see when we go to the cinema are featherless and that's not what most were like,' he says. 'Also, some dinosaurs in movies have poisonous bites, but there's no evidence to suggest that was ever the case. In fact, I think it's highly unlikely.'

Palaeontology is a fast-moving field with new discoveries being made all the time. Fossils are regularly found, and previously unknown species are identified. Experts are continuing to investigate issues of great importance. 'We still don't know much about how dinosaurs originally developed,' says James. 'It's something I'd be very keen to do some work on if the opportunity arose.'

Imagine you are going to give a talk about dinosaurs and the dinosaur expert to your classmates.

Use words from the article to help you write some notes.

Make short notes under each heading.

Question 8

How movie dinosaurs are different from the real dinosaurs:

Example: *move much faster*

- ....
- ....
- ....
- .... [4]

Question 9

Questions about dinosaurs that James would like to do more research on:

- ....
- ....
- .... [3]

[Total: 7]

Exercise 4

Read the article about children who use their imagination to invent friends, and then answer the questions.

IMAGINARY FRIENDS

Rachael Parker's childhood friend Michael wasn't real; he was the product of her imagination.

When I was a little girl, I had a very good friend called Michael. He wasn't a real boy, but he felt very real to me. We played and talked for hours on end. Unlike me, he was brave, confident and badly behaved – that sort of detail is still amazingly fresh in my mind. My mum and dad knew all about him, and, for a while, they even put a plate of food out for him at mealtimes, as my mum recently reminded me. She also said she thought he had come into my life when I was five and left when I was eight.

Over the years, I've often wondered if I was unusual or if having an imaginary friend was an aspect of growing up found all over the world, and I eventually thought I should try to find the answer from various studies carried out in recent years. It turns out that, historically at least, 50% of all children everywhere have had invisible companions. I also came across some other interesting facts. For example, first born and only children are most likely to have imaginary friends, but roughly equal numbers of boys and girls seem to have them. Something else that caught my attention is that there appears to be a decline in the number of children with imaginary friends, possibly due to increased time spent looking at electronic devices.

So, what are imaginary friends for? Do children make them up just in order to avoid feeling lonely? To have someone to play with at any time? 'One thing I have learned from a series of studies I have been involved with is that no single explanation fits all children,' says psychologist Tessa Francis. 'Small children vary enormously and imaginary friends come in many different shapes and sizes. They serve many different functions, with loneliness avoidance being just one, though perhaps the best-known, among **them**.' Interestingly, very young children often create a fantasy figure to take the blame for bad behaviour.

In my case, Michael was responsible for emptying the biscuit tin on at least one occasion. He also used to make a terrible mess in my bedroom, as I explained to my mum, and he refused to tidy it up too.

Some children use an imaginary friend to help them deal with awkward situations. 'Children who are scared because it's dark may turn to their imaginary friends for support,' says Dr Francis. 'Or I've seen cases where a child has a difficult day at school but keeps this from their parents, and when they get home, they immediately start playing with their imaginary friend. This is to take their minds off what has upset them, but the parents may well be unaware of this. Parents expect their children to tell them about any problems they may have, but unfortunately things are often not that straightforward.'

Some studies of children with imaginary friends have found them to be more creative than other children. Other studies have found they are better at putting themselves in other people's shoes. Does this mean that having an imaginary friend will give you greater creativity and social awareness? If so, should imaginary friends be encouraged? Some psychologists say that children who are already creative and socially aware may be more likely to invent fantasy figures, but further studies are needed to resolve these issues. They have a point. That said, it seems safe to assume that playing and communicating with a made-up person is hardly likely to damage a child's social and creative abilities. Far from it.

Question 10

When thinking about her imaginary childhood friend, the writer is surprised at

A   how long her relationship with him lasted.

B   how clearly she remembers what he was like.

C   how much interest her parents showed in him. [1]

Question 11

What question made the writer decide to read about research focussing on imaginary friends?

A   why certain children have them while others don't

B   whether as many children today as in the past have them

C   how common it is for children to have them [1]

Question 12

What does 'them' in line 22 refer to?

A   reasons for having imaginary friends

B   investigations into the topic of imaginary friends

C   different types of imaginary friends that children have [1]

Question 13

What is the writer doing in paragraph 4?

A   putting forward her own views

B   using examples to explain a point

C   introducing a new topic [1]

Question 14

According to Dr Francis in paragraph 5, parents sometimes

A fail to realise why their children feel the need for imaginary friends. ☐

B find it hard to talk to their children about imaginary friends. ☐

C feel unsure whether it's good for their children to have imaginary friends. ☐ [1]

Question 15

What point does the writer make in the final paragraph?

A Experts disagree on the best way to describe imaginary friends. ☐

B Having imaginary friends will probably help children develop certain skills. ☐

C Research strongly indicates that children with imaginary friends have similar personality types. ☐ [1]

[Total: 6]

Exercise 5
Question 16

You recently helped to organise a special celebration at your school.

Write an email to a friend explaining what happened.

In your email, you should:

- explain what the celebration was for
- describe how you helped to organise the celebration
- say why you think it is important for schools to organise celebrations.

Write about 120 to 160 words.

You will receive up to 6 marks for the content of your email, and up to 9 marks for the language used.

[Total: 15]

Exercise 6

Question 17

A local newspaper is planning to publish reviews of books that are good for young people to read. You decide to write a review of a book that you and some of your friends have read.

In your review, explain what the book is about and say why you think other young people should read it.

Here are some comments from your friends who have read the book:

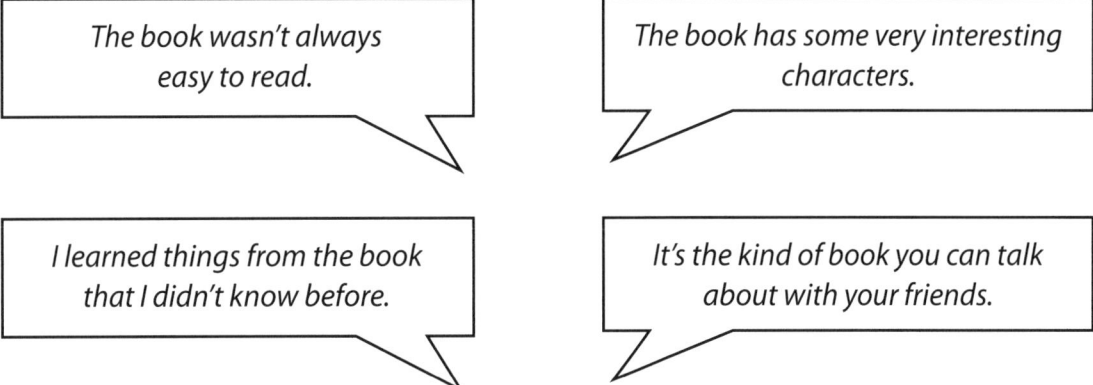

Now write a review for the newspaper.

The comments above may give you some ideas, and you should also use some ideas of your own.

Write about 120 to 160 words.

You will receive up to 6 marks for the content of your review, and up to 9 marks for the language used.

[Total: 15]

Practice Test 1

Listening

Exercise 1

 You will hear eight short recordings. For each question, choose the correct answer, **A**, **B**, **C** or **D**, and put a tick (✔) in the appropriate box.

You will hear each recording twice.

Question 1

What new thing does the girl have in her room?

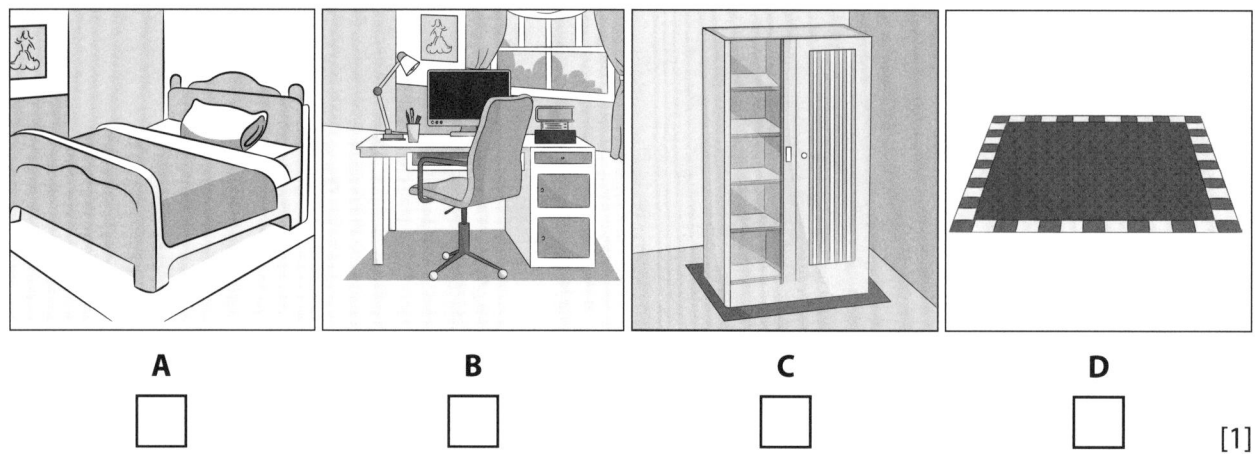

[1]

Question 2

What does the boy plan to draw next?

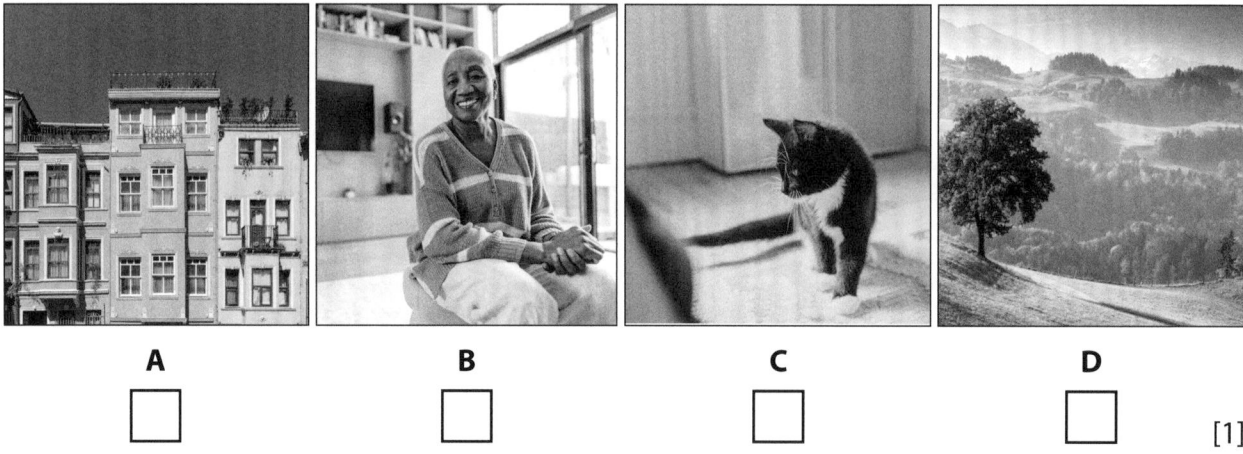

[1]

Audio for the listening exercises is available in the digital resource.

Question 3

What did the girl help her aunt with at her new house?

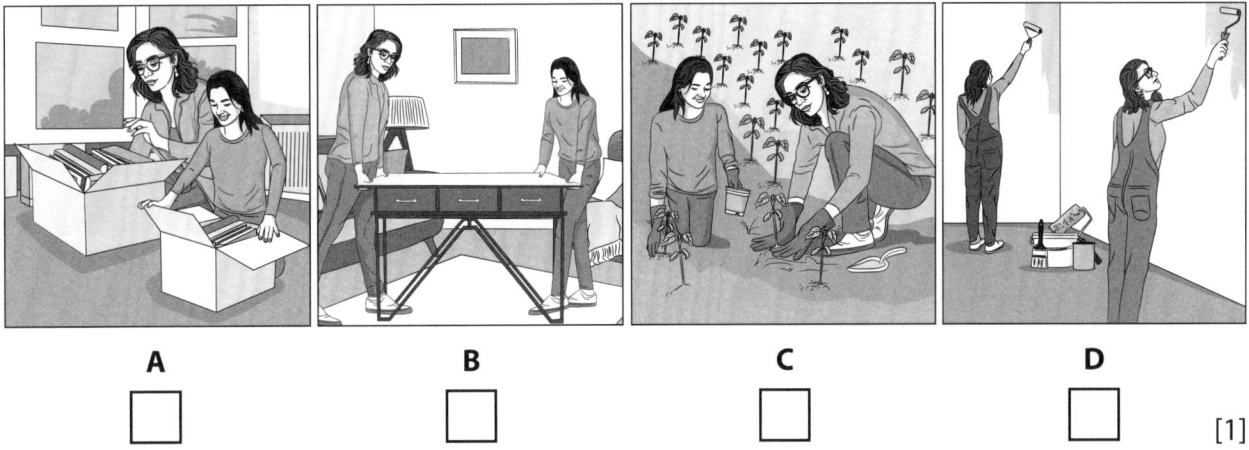

A B C D [1]

Question 4

What kind of film did the boy's family watch on Saturday?

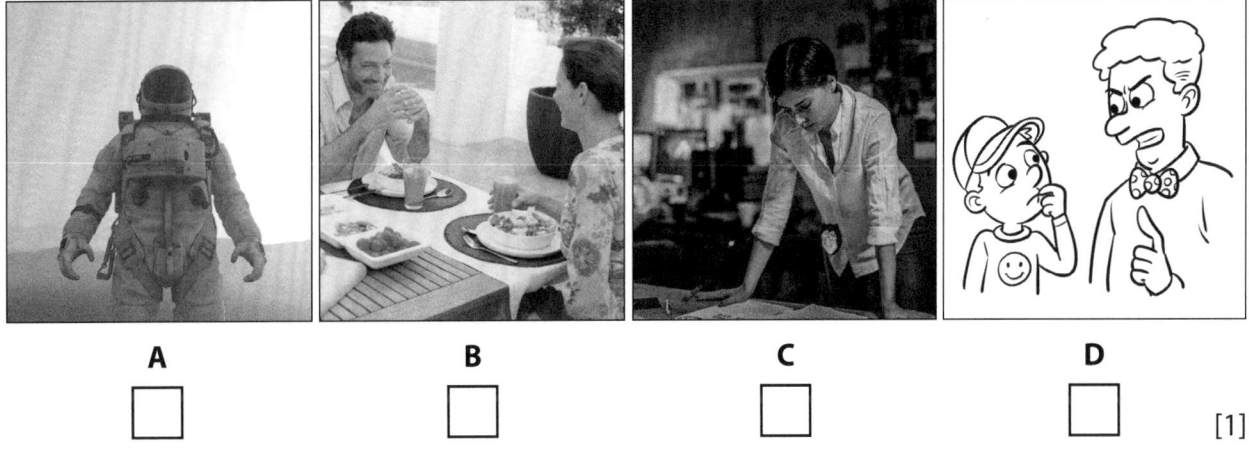

A B C D [1]

Audio for the listening exercises is available in the digital resource.

Question 5

What activity will the girl try with her family next weekend?

Question 6

What problem did the boy have at school today?

Audio for the listening exercises is available in the digital resource.

Question 7

How did the man get to work on Friday?

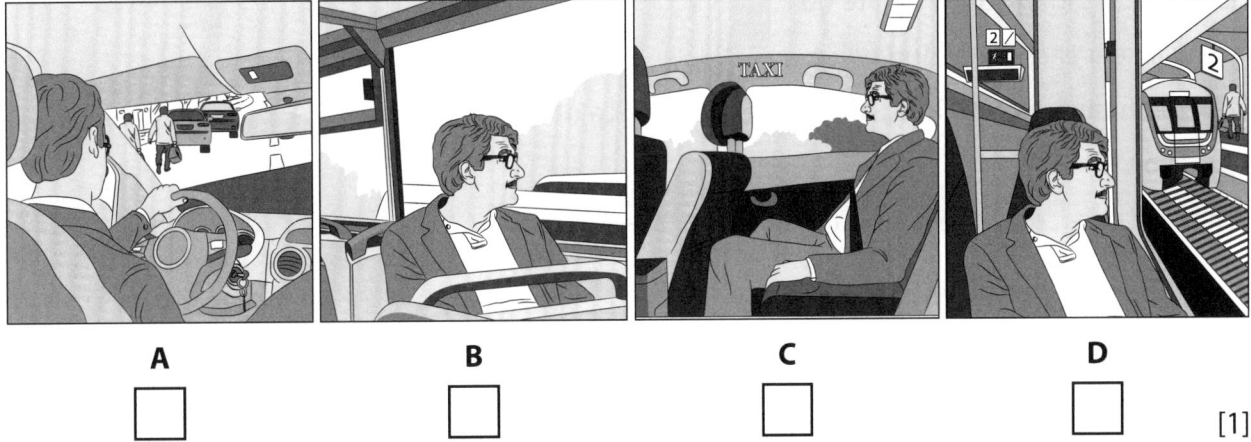

A ☐   B ☐   C ☐   D ☐   [1]

Question 8

What did the boy cook for his family?

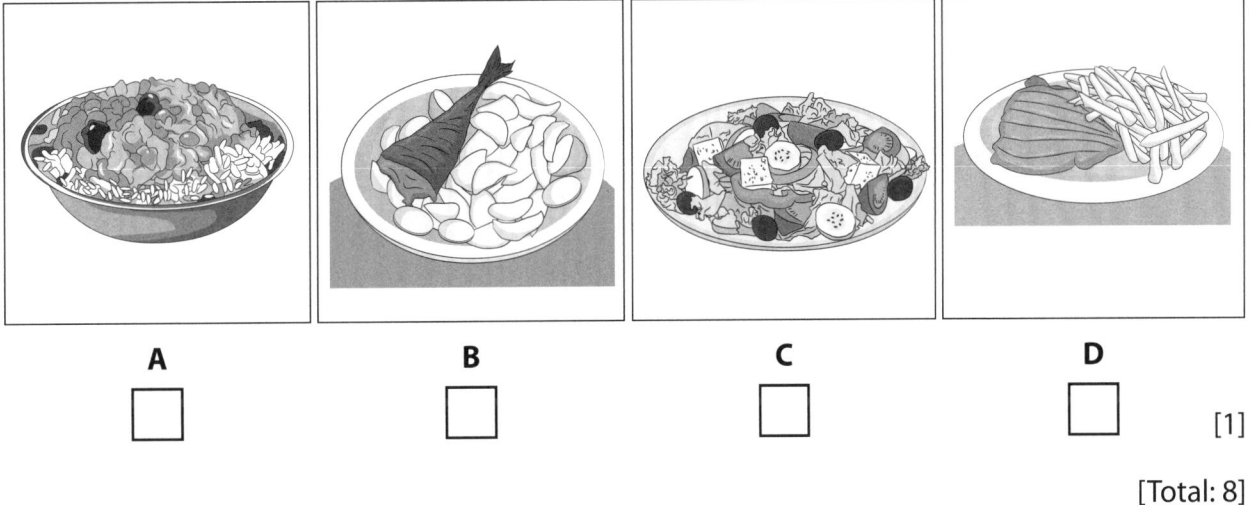

A ☐   B ☐   C ☐   D ☐   [1]

[Total: 8]

Audio for the listening exercises is available in the digital resource.

Exercise 2

You will hear five short recordings. For each question, choose the correct answer, **A**, **B** or **C**, and put a tick (✔) in the appropriate box.

You will hear each recording twice.

You will hear a man talking about his experience of running a race.

Question 9

What was the man worried about before the race?

A noise from the spectators

B making a good start

C the weather conditions   [1]

Question 10

What does the man think is the reason for his good result?

A He made changes to his diet.

B He worked hard to make sure he was ready.

C He took advice from someone more experienced.   [1]

Audio for the listening exercises is available in the digital resource.

You will hear a girl talking about her favourite singer.

Question 11

What does the girl think is special about her favourite singer?

A the variety in her music ☐

B the emotion she communicates ☐

C the subjects she sings about ☐   [1]

Question 12

Why was the girl disappointed by her favourite singer's concert?

A the venue was too dark ☐

B the sound quality was poor ☐

C the choice of songs was limited ☐   [1]

You will hear a girl talking about organising a party for her grandfather.

Question 13

What does the girl say was difficult about organising the birthday party?

A buying food ☐

B choosing a date ☐

C agreeing on a venue ☐   [1]

Question 14

What pleased her grandad most about the party?

A the dancing ☐

B receiving surprise gifts ☐

C seeing his friends ☐   [1]

Audio for the listening exercises is available in the digital resource.

You will hear a boy talking about his new part-time job.

Question 15

What surprised the boy about his new job?

A   how little training he was given

B   how tiring it was

C   how unhelpful his colleagues were   [1]

Question 16

The boy hopes that he will soon

A   meet the boss.

B   get more money.

C   change his working hours.   [1]

You will hear a girl talking about doing a history project for school.

Question 17

What does the girl say was most challenging about the project?

A   having enough time to do it

B   working with her classmates

C   finding reliable information   [1]

Question 18

How did the teacher feel about the girl's project?

A   impressed by the artwork

B   surprised she had written so much

C   pleased with the final section   [1]

[Total: 10]

Audio for the listening exercises is available in the digital resource.

Exercise 3

 You will hear a science teacher giving a talk about asteroids, which are small rocky objects found mostly between the planets Mars and Jupiter. For each question, choose the correct answer, **A**, **B** or **C**, and put a tick (✔) in the appropriate box.

You will hear the talk twice.

Now look at questions **19–26**.

Asteroids

Question 19

Asteroids are most commonly known as

A planetoids. ☐

B minor planets. ☐

C dwarf planets. ☐ [1]

Question 20

The speaker is surprised that some asteroids have

A moons. ☐

B tails. ☐

C rings. ☐ [1]

Audio for the listening exercises is available in the digital resource.

Question 21

The most common type of asteroid is … in colour.

A red ☐

B green ☐

C grey ☐ [1]

Question 22

The speaker dislikes the fact that some asteroids are named after

A places on Earth. ☐

B mythological characters. ☐

C celebrities. ☐ [1]

Question 23

An asteroid becomes a threat to the Earth when it measures at least

A 30 metres. ☐

B 10 metres. ☐

C 50 kilometres. ☐ [1]

Question 24

The 2006 spacecraft that visited an asteroid was important because it was the first to

A land on the surface. ☐

B collect rock samples. ☐

C take photographs. ☐ [1]

Audio for the listening exercises is available in the digital resource.

Question 25

The speaker was amazed that … could be mined on asteroids one day.

A tin

B iron

C gold [1]

Question 26

Elements found on asteroids could also be used to produce

A rocket fuel.

B ice.

C oxygen. [1]

[Total: 8]

Audio for the listening exercises is available in the digital resource.

Exercise 4

 You will hear six students talking about experiments they did in science lessons.

For questions **27–32**, choose from the list (**A–H**) showing which idea each speaker expresses. Write the correct letter (**A–H**) on the answer line. Use each letter only once. There are two extra letters which you do not need to use.

You will hear the recordings twice.

Now read statements **A–H**.

| A | I wish I'd listened to advice from my friends. |

| B | Working with others proved more fun than expected. |

| C | I found the work very challenging. |

| D | I was surprised by the good results. |

| E | It took a long time to prepare everything. |

| F | It has changed my attitude to science. |

| G | The mistakes I made weren't too serious. |

| H | The equipment didn't work properly. |

Question 27	Speaker 1	[1]
Question 28	Speaker 2	[1]
Question 29	Speaker 3	[1]
Question 30	Speaker 4	[1]
Question 31	Speaker 5	[1]
Question 32	Speaker 6	[1]

[Total: 6]

Audio for the listening exercises is available in the digital resource.

Exercise 5

You will hear an interview with a woman called Jo Baylis, who is a radio presenter. For each question, choose the correct answer, **A**, **B** or **C**, and put a tick (✔) in the appropriate box.

You will hear the interview twice.

Now look at questions **33–40**.

Question 33

Jo decided to become a radio presenter because

A she was excited about an experience her father had.

B she believed that she had the right personality for it.

C she loved a particular radio programme. [1]

Question 34

What does Jo say about her first experience of being on the radio?

A She had too little time to prepare before her first show.

B She was disappointed by the lack of training offered.

C She was too anxious to perform well. [1]

Question 35

Jo prefers to present programmes which focus on

A discussing different topics.

B introducing new music.

C reviewing films and TV programmes. [1]

Question 36

What does Jo say about having to get up early in the morning to present her show?

A She needs time to get herself into the right mood.

B She has overcome her initial problems with it.

C She regrets the effect it has on her social life. [1]

Audio for the listening exercises is available in the digital resource.

Question 37

What does Jo say about the comments she gets from her listeners?

A She tries to respond to all the points people make. ☐

B She wishes people would try to be more positive. ☐

C She is surprised by the range of opinions people have. ☐ [1]

Question 38

What does Jo say is the most difficult aspect of her job?

A coming up with new ideas for each programme ☐

B having to maintain a high level of concentration ☐

C having to do so many different things ☐ [1]

Question 39

According to Jo, when she presents a programme, she

A has to think carefully about the impression she wants to give. ☐

B sometimes feels uncomfortable about not seeing her audience. ☐

C imagines she is talking to a group of her friends. ☐ [1]

Question 40

Jo doubts that she will ever become a TV presenter because

A she is afraid she might not be successful at it. ☐

B she wants to improve her skills in her current job. ☐

C she thinks it is unlikely she would be offered work. ☐ [1]

[Total: 8]

Audio for the listening exercises is available in the digital resource.

Speaking

How to use the speaking practice tests

To carry out the speaking practice tests, you will need someone else to take on the role of examiner. There are two copies provided for each test – an examiner copy containing guidance on carrying out the test and a student copy containing a speaking assessment card. The student should not look at their card until told to do so by the examiner.

The examiner may wish to use a timer. The test could also be recorded, in order to replay it afterwards.

For further guidance on how to develop ideas in the speaking sections in Practice Tests 1–3, please refer to the Answer key section. There you will find suggestions for the following:

Practice Test 1

- how to develop ideas in part 1 (interview)
- how to develop ideas in part 2 (short talk)
- how to develop ideas in part 3 (discussion)

Practice Test 2

- how to develop ideas in part 2 (short talk)
- how to develop ideas in part 3 (discussion)

Practice Test 3

- how to develop ideas in part 3 (discussion)

Examiner copy: Practice Test 1 – Speaking

Warm-up (1–2 minutes)

Put the student at ease by conducting a short conversation using the following questions:

- Where do you usually do your homework?
- What place would you like to visit during your next holiday?
- How did you meet your best friend?

Part 1 – Interview (2–3 minutes)

Tell the student the topic for this part (healthy lifestyle). Conduct a short interview with the student by asking the following questions. If the student does not know how to answer the question, ask the question again. If the student still does not know what to say, move on to the next question.

Healthy lifestyle

- How do people keep fit nowadays?
- Can you tell me about the last time you spent some time outdoors?
- Do you think it is easy to lead a healthy lifestyle nowadays? Why? Why not?

Part 2 – Short talk (3–4 minutes including 1 minute preparation time)

Ask the student to look at their speaking assessment card, which contains the following information. The student has up to 1 minute to read the card and prepare for the talk. The student cannot make any written notes. After one minute, ask the student to start their short talk.

Learning a new skill

You are planning to learn something new this year. You are considering the following options:

- cycling
- playing a musical instrument.

Discuss what is easy or difficult about learning each skill. Say which skill you would prefer to learn, and why.

Part 3 – Discussion (3–4 minutes)

Conduct a discussion using the following questions. If the student says very little, encourage a further discussion by asking questions like, *Why do you think so?*, *Can you tell me a bit more about …?*, etc. If the student does not know what to say, give them a few seconds, then move on to the next question.

- Do you think that teenagers have enough time for their hobbies nowadays?
- Some people say that roads are not safe for cyclists these days. What is your opinion?
- Is listening to music a good way to relax? What do you think?
- There is an opinion that being a musician isn't a good career choice for young people. Would you agree?

Student copy: Practice Test 1 – Speaking

IMPORTANT: Do not look at this card until the examiner tells you to.

Speaking assessment card

Learning a new skill

You are planning to learn something new this year. You are considering the following options:

- cycling
- playing a musical instrument.

Discuss what is easy or difficult about learning each skill. Say which skill you would prefer to learn, and why.

Practice Test 2
Reading and Writing

Exercise 1

Read the article about a young artist called Hamzah Yusuf, and then answer the questions.

HAMZAH YUSUF – TEENAGE ARTIST

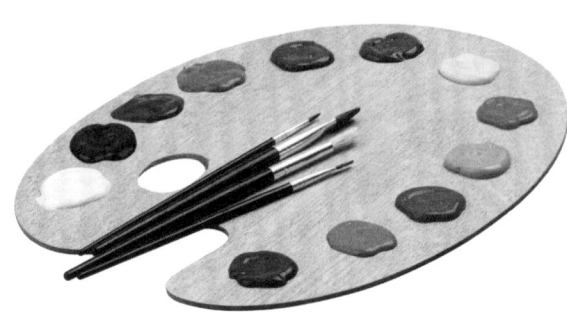

Like many other 13-year-old boys, Hamzah Yusuf loves playing basketball with his friends. In other ways, though, he is very different from most boys his age. Since the age of seven, when some of his drawings and paintings were first exhibited, his special talents have been widely recognised.

Hamzah started drawing when he turned six after one of his uncles gave him a sketchpad and some coloured pencils, brushes and paints. His father, Musa, and his mother, Parveen, own a clothes shop. 'Hamzah basically taught himself to draw and paint,' Parveen says. 'I'm not sure where he gets his ability from.' She designs some of the clothes they sell, but claims she isn't very artistic. It wasn't long before Hamzah was invited to contribute to an exhibition in a local gallery – something he was very happy to do. Musa and Parveen were astonished when they found out that the gallery had sold all of his work within a few days.

'Nowadays, lots of people are interested in Hamzah's drawings and paintings,' his father says. 'And lots want to buy them. But the attention and money haven't really affected him. He isn't into that sort of thing.' In fact, Hamzah has a simple lifestyle. He rarely goes on social media, and has little interest in video games, unlike most of his friends. He's a fan of skateboarding – he mainly does that in his local park – but what he likes most is to work on his art, although he does take pleasure in listening to music while painting. While he has recently produced a few portraits of individuals he knows, urban scenes have always been the focus of the majority of his work.

Hamzah paints quickly and completes over a hundred paintings every year. How does he manage it? He realises he has a rare gift, and this gives him considerable self-confidence. The key, as he sees it, though, is his determination. 'I make lots of mistakes and face problems all the time when I'm painting,' he says. 'I sometimes spend hours trying to sort something out in a picture I'm doing and it's still wrong. That used to really annoy me but I've now worked out what to do.' He leaves the picture for a day. Then, when he comes back to it, a solution usually comes to him. After completing a picture, he feels the need to do something different and he often spends time learning magic tricks. 'I'm not confident enough to perform in public yet,' he says, 'but maybe I will one day.' If he's anywhere near as good at it as he is at painting, he'll be worth watching.

Question 1

How old was Hamzah when his art began to attract public attention?

.... [1]

Question 2

How did Hamzah's parents feel when people started to buy his paintings?

.... [1]

Question 3

What is the main subject of Hamzah's paintings?

.... [1]

Question 4

What does Hamzah believe is the most important quality he has?

.... [1]

Question 5

What does Hamzah do when he cannot make progress with a painting?

.... [1]

Question 6

What hobbies apart from art does Hamzah have? Give **three** details.

....

....

.... [3]

[Total: 8]

Exercise 2

Read extracts from a magazine article in which four students (**A–D**) write about working as volunteers on archaeological projects. Then answer Question **7(a)–(i)**.

VOLUNTEERS ON ARCHAEOLOGICAL PROJECTS

A   Abdi Hassan

Last summer, my friend Sara asked me if I'd like to work with her on an archaeological project in Italy. She'd wanted to do something similar for ages, but was nervous about going there alone. We ended up having such an interesting time that I'm thinking about doing it again next year. All the volunteers were based in a student residence, and we helped archaeologists investigate the remains of some 3000-year-old buildings. We dug up bits of ancient tiles, pottery and bones, and cleaned them carefully using special knives and brushes. The archaeologists in charge were great at explaining things and keeping everyone happy. It was too hot to do anything in the afternoons, so we got up at 4 a.m. while it was cool, and worked through the morning. Then we did more in the evenings. It was really tough. I eventually adapted to things, but it took me a while.

B   Angela Choo

Earlier this year, I spent a month as a volunteer on an archaeological project in Peru. If I'd known how brilliant it would be, I'd have arranged to spend another month there, but that wasn't possible in the end, unfortunately. Along with other volunteers, I helped archaeologists to investigate and conserve some remains from the Inca civilisation. We mostly had to clear away trees and other plants that had grown on the sites. We did it with saws and huge knives called machetes. Using these might look quite straightforward, but it wasn't, as I soon realised. Working high in the Andes mountains was tough. There's less oxygen up there, so it can be hard to breathe, which was a shock initially, but I loved my time there. One day, I actually found a piece of Inca jewellery. The archaeologists kept it to examine more closely, but finding it was such a thrill.

C   Raul Valencia

I'm an archaeology student and I've worked as a volunteer on several different projects. The most recent was on Orkney Island off the north coast of Scotland, where there are some important remains of 5000-year-old Stone Age settlements. Working on a Stone Age site was a dream of mine and actually getting to do it was great, especially because some well-known and respected archaeologists run the project. As I already had some archaeological experience, I didn't just do the basic work; they asked me to take measurements of Stone Age walls, and record objects that people had discovered, which was quite complicated sometimes. There are lots of really interesting ancient objects buried under the ground there. It can get very windy, wet and cold on Orkney, and you could never describe the hostel where the volunteers stay as comfortable, but it's a beautiful, fascinating place which is definitely worth visiting.

D Kirstin Michaels

I spent two weeks working on some ancient Roman ruins in Bulgaria. Our living quarters were simple but clean, and I can't imagine anyone not falling in love with the place. It was the first time I'd ever travelled to a different country by myself, and there had been a few questions on my mind, like: What if the people are unfriendly? What if I don't like the food? But everything was wonderful, even on days when all I did was use a spade and a fork to dig large holes so the researchers could see what lay under the surface. I knew they might come across some valuable historical evidence down there. I'm not particularly suited to that kind of heavy work, but I think I did a good job. In fact, the head archaeologist thanked me and said I'd done more than many volunteers manage in twice the time.

For each question write the correct letter A, B, C or D on the line.

Question 7

Which person…

(a) is pleased to have been able to fulfil an ambition? .... [1]

(b) mentions finding the daily schedule hard to get used to? .... [1]

(c) regrets not staying on the project longer? .... [1]

(d) feels proud of a physical achievement? .... [1]

(e) mentions the difficulty of working with certain tools? .... [1]

(f) feels inspired to do more archaeological work in future? .... [1]

(g) admits to being anxious before joining the project? .... [1]

(h) suggests that some people might dislike the accommodation at the site? .... [1]

(i) praises the skills of the project leaders? .... [1]

[Total: 9]

Exercise 3

Read the article about space debris, which is rubbish that has been left by humans in space, and then complete the notes.

SPACE DEBRIS

In August 2016, engineers at the European Space Agency (ESA) realised that something was wrong with their most important observation satellite – it had been hit by a tiny piece of debris. 'It could have been something like a piece of soap,' says one engineer. 'All sorts of things have been left in space and they travel at extremely high speeds. I've seen images of drops of unused fuel in orbit.' Fortunately, the engineers were able to carry out repairs, but the incident was a reminder that one day a very expensive piece of technology could be destroyed by space litter.

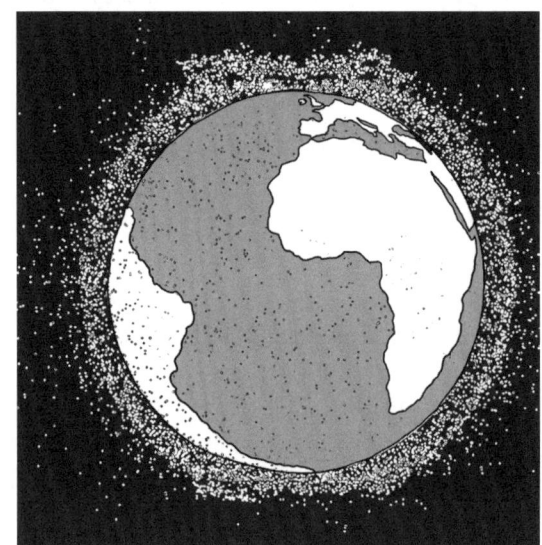

Out of more than 5000 satellites sent into space since the very first one was launched in the 1950s, only about 1200 of them are currently working; the rest just orbit the earth like large pieces of junk. In addition, there are thought to be 150 million tiny bits of human litter floating around in space. Old batteries have been reported, and while they may not seem significant, they can be very dangerous.

'There's so much debris,' says one ESA engineer. 'It can be as small as bits of paint. Some sections of space may eventually become unusable.' Scientists at the ESA are currently working on so-called robotic space vacuum cleaners. They also have plans for spacecraft which function as space garbage trucks to pick up rubbish. Projects like this are costly and difficult, however.

'Satellites and other spacecraft are equipped with radars which detect large objects, so they can avoid them,' says the ESA engineer. 'But the systems can't always detect objects of a more limited scale – like a tool lost by an astronaut during a spacewalk. Things like that can put human life at risk. Don't forget that there are people working on the International Space Station and in other spacecraft.'

There are plans to launch several thousand new satellites within the next few years to provide improved communications and internet access for all parts of the world. This makes the need to deal with space debris even more urgent. One possible solution involves satellites designed to automatically return to earth.

Dealing with smaller waste is, in some ways, more difficult. A research project in the USA is aiming to develop laser beams to get rid of the orbiting rubbish. Another project in Japan is building a giant net to collect small objects over a period of time.

Some of the ideas being considered are hard to imagine, but solutions for dealing with the litter that humans leave in space are clearly needed.

Imagine you are going to give a talk about space debris to your class at school.

Use words from the article to help you write some notes.

Make short notes under each heading.

Question 8

Examples of small pieces of space debris:

Example: *a piece of soap*

- ....
- ....
- .... [3]

Question 9

Ideas for removing space debris:

- ....
- ....
- ....
- .... [4]

[Total: 7]

Exercise 4

Read the article about a sport in which people run up the stairs in very tall buildings, and then answer the questions.

TOWER RUNNING

Ben Wright takes part in a race which involves running up one of London's tallest buildings

I'd partly run and partly walked to floor 18 of the 35-storey skyscraper, halfway through the first stage of the race, and already my lungs and legs were hurting badly. As a 26-year-old regular cyclist and tennis player, why was this so painful? Was I capable of reaching the top floor, and then doing the whole thing twice more to finish the race? Surely my body would fail me and I'd have to quit. Then I heard the footsteps of two runners three floors below. They're probably 20 years older than me, I thought. I can't let them catch up. That wouldn't look good.

Four weeks earlier, Jenny, a fellow teacher in my college, had asked me to sponsor her. 'I'm raising money for a medical charity,' she said. 'It'll mean climbing 880 stairs three times. I've been training for two weeks and it's tough, even for people in great shape.' I've always preferred outdoor sports, but the idea of racing up the concrete staircase of a skyscraper in the heart of London suddenly seemed very appealing, and I felt I had to try it for myself. So, I signed up for the same event as Jenny.

There's lots of information online about tower running. The first recognised race was in 1978, up the 1576 steps of the Empire State Building in New York. The sport then grew steadily as skyscrapers went up all over the planet, and as real estate companies saw funding tower running as a way of promoting their businesses. Nowadays, there's a tower running championship with more than 150 events per year in over 25 different countries. It's incredible to think that, in theory, you could run in three events every week of the year.

I recently discovered that one of my neighbours, Anya, is a keen tower runner. 'A group of us enter races together and we've become good friends,' Anya told me. She used to run marathons, but was always getting injured. 'Someone told me that running up steps was kinder on the hips, knees and ankles. So, I gave it a go and I've been injury free ever since.' Anya trains after work on the stairs leading up to her 12th floor office. 'When I was doing marathons, I trained for 20 hours a week. I do half that now, but it's so intensive that I'm as fit as ever.'

Anya was happy to pass on some tips. 'Take two steps, rather than one, with each stride,' she suggested. It's more tiring, but once I'd established a rhythm, I managed to keep going and it made a significant difference to my speed. Anya also warned me against looking down at the steps. 'Over time, bending forward can cause back pain.' Fortunately, my natural running style is upright, so this wasn't really an issue for me, but what I did find awkward was using the handrail to pull myself up. 'Your arms take some of the load off your legs that way,' Anya pointed out. 'Some people find it easier than others, though.' I was clearly one of the latter.

The last set of steps took me up to a beautiful roof garden. My watch said I'd only taken seven minutes to get there, though it had felt much longer. From 35 floors up, the views of the city spread out below – in contrast to the burning sensations affecting my legs and chest – were absolutely wonderful. With two more full climbs of the tower still to do, however, I couldn't hang around and fully appreciate **them**. So, I walked to the lift, sped down to the ground floor and started all over again.

Question 10

Halfway through the first stage of the race, the writer was

A worried he would be overtaken by other competitors.

B aware that he needed to adopt a different approach.

C tempted by the idea of giving up. [1]

Question 11

What was the writer's main reason for entering the race?

A to support a colleague

B to test his physical fitness

C to find out what the experience was like [1]

Question 12

What was the writer particularly impressed to learn about tower running?

A how long people have been doing it

B how many races there are worldwide

C how much financial backing it receives [1]

Question 13

Why did the writer's neighbour switch from running on flat ground to tower running?

A It is less time consuming.

B It is a more sociable activity.

C It puts less strain on her body. [1]

Question 14

What advice about tower running did the writer find most helpful?

A Keep your head up when you run.

B Make full use of the handrail.

C Climb two steps at a time. [1]

Question 15

What does 'them' in line 35 refer to?

A views

B sensations

C climbs [1]

[Total: 6]

Exercise 5
Question 16

You recently went on a class visit to a museum.

Write an email to a friend about the visit.

In your email, you should:

- describe the museum that you went to
- explain what you liked most about the museum
- say how the museum could attract more young people.

Write about 120 to 160 words.

You will receive up to 6 marks for the content of your email, and up to 9 marks for the language used.

[Total: 15]

Exercise 6

Question 17

Your class has recently been studying different environmental problems. Your teacher has asked you to write a report about an environmental issue in your school.

In your report, describe something about the school that you think is bad for the environment and suggest what could be done to improve the situation.

Here are some comments from other students in your class:

- *A lot of electricity is wasted.*
- *There aren't many trees in the school grounds.*
- *Regular activities to pick up litter around the school would be good.*
- *People talk about environmental problems but they don't do anything about them.*

Now write a report for your teacher.

The comments above may give you some ideas, and you should also use some ideas of your own.

Write about 120 to 160 words.

You will receive up to 6 marks for the content of your report, and up to 9 marks for the language used.

....
....
....
....
....
....
....
....
....

[Total: 15]

Practice Test 2

Listening

Exercise 1

 You will hear eight short recordings. For each question, choose the correct answer, **A, B, C** or **D**, and put a tick (✔) in the appropriate box.

You will hear each recording twice.

Question 1

What subject is the girl's online blog about?

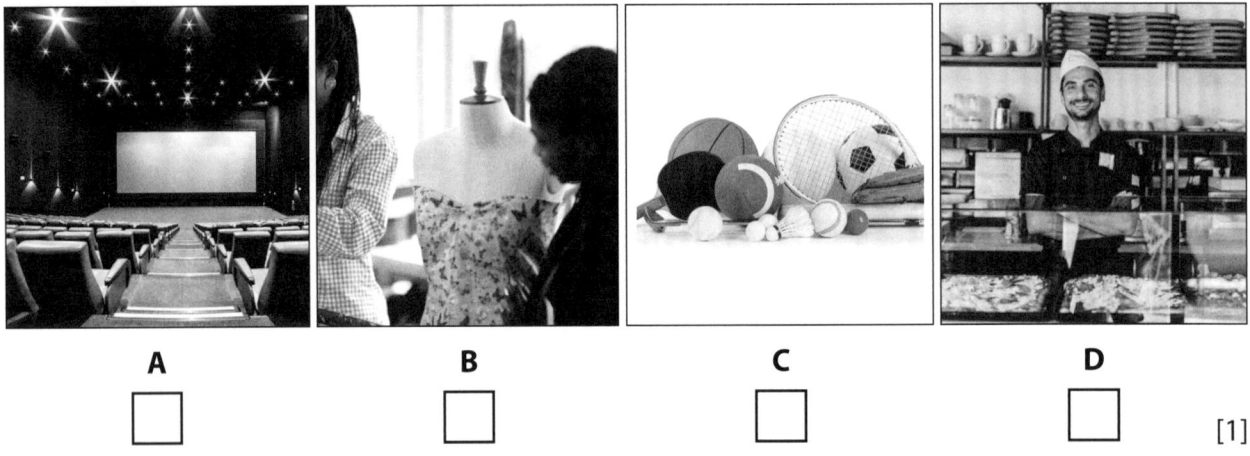

A ☐   B ☐   C ☐   D ☐ [1]

Question 2

How is the girl's father planning to celebrate his birthday this year?

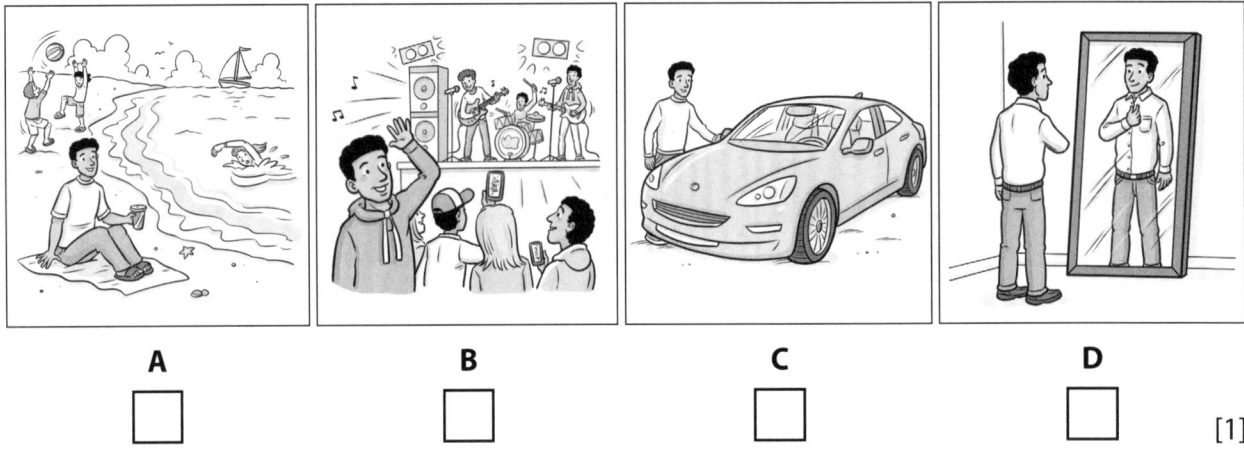

A ☐   B ☐   C ☐   D ☐ [1]

Audio for the listening exercises is available in the digital resource.

Question 3

What is the boy's geography project about?

A ☐   B ☐   C ☐   D ☐   [1]

Question 4

What new skill would the girl like to learn?

A ☐   B ☐   C ☐   D ☐   [1]

Audio for the listening exercises is available in the digital resource.

Question 5

What did the man have problems with today?

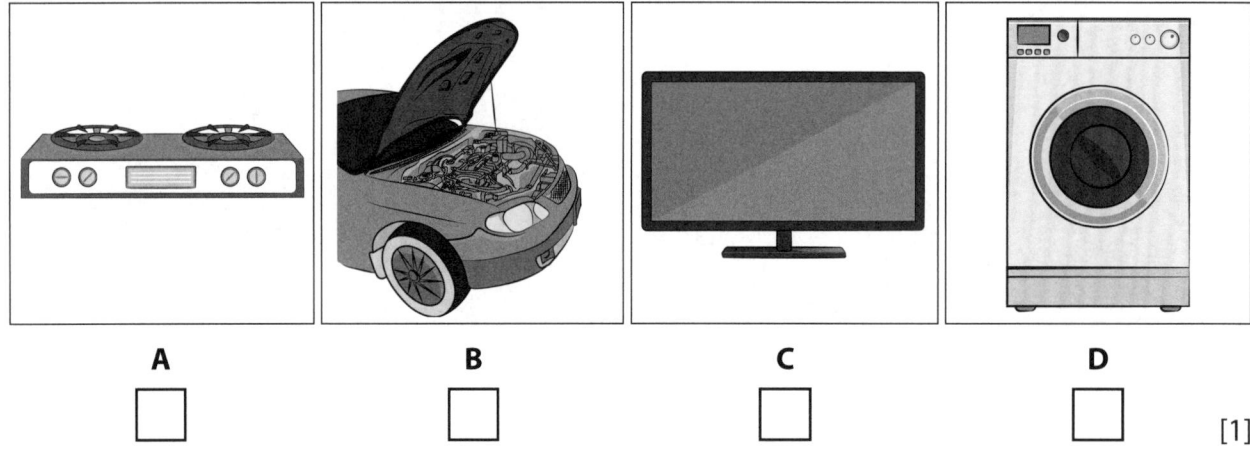

A B C D [1]

Question 6

Where did the girl spend time with her friend today?

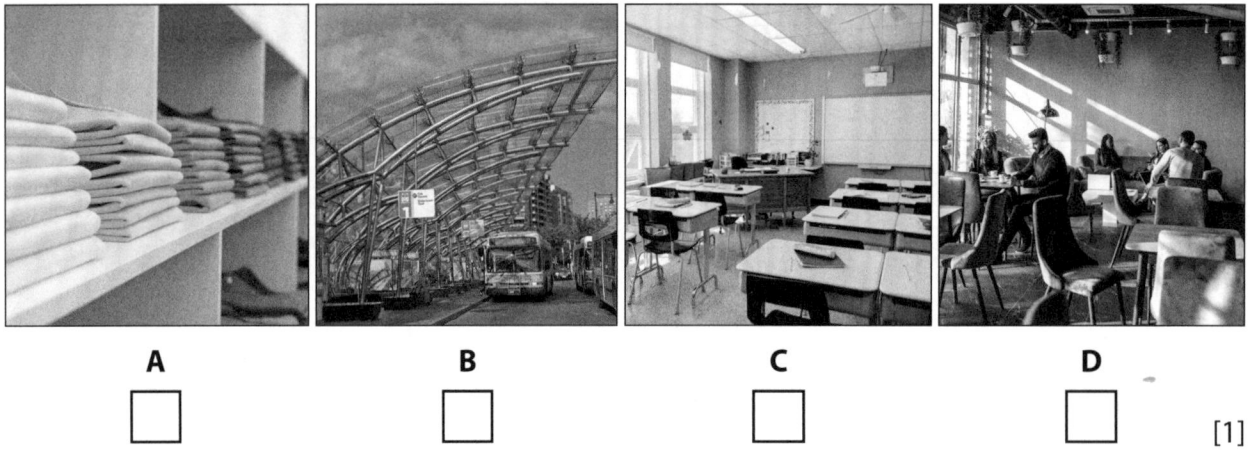

A B C D [1]

Audio for the listening exercises is available in the digital resource.

Question 7

What new thing did the man need to get for his holiday in the United States?

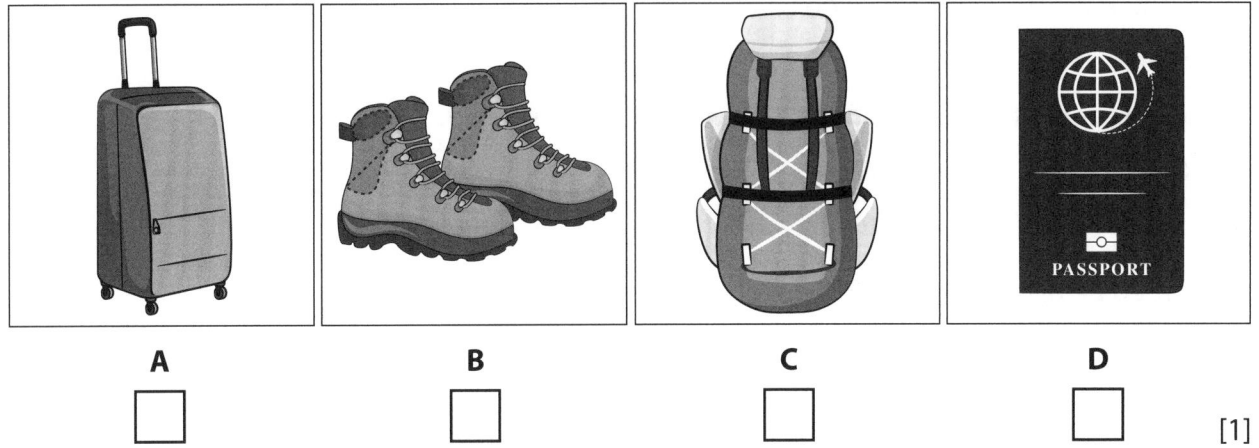

A ☐　　B ☐　　C ☐　　D ☐ [1]

Question 8

Who does the girl think will win the talent show?

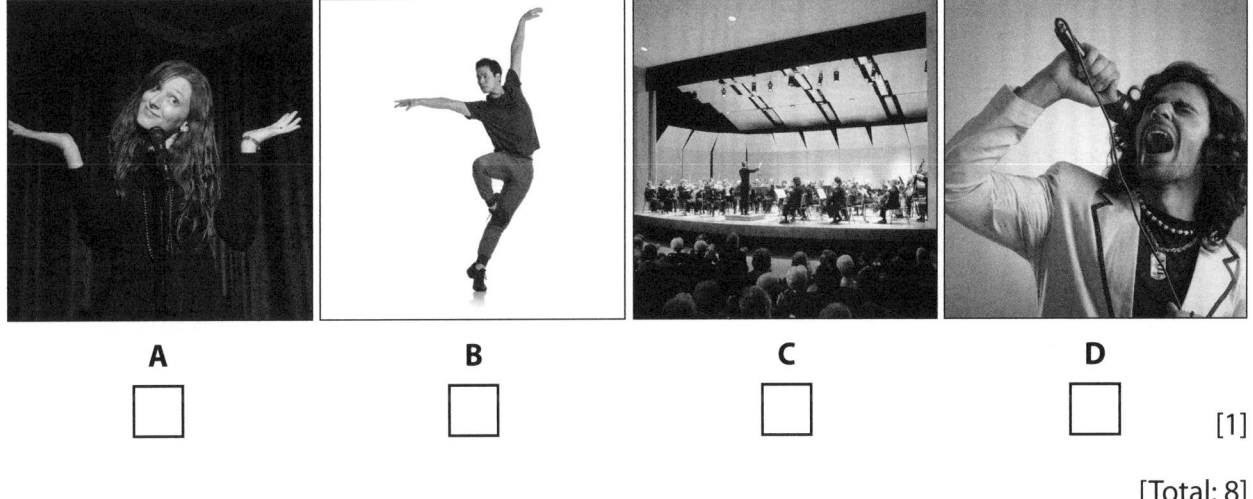

A ☐　　B ☐　　C ☐　　D ☐ [1]

[Total: 8]

Audio for the listening exercises is available in the digital resource.

Exercise 2

 You will hear five short recordings. For each question, choose the correct answer, **A**, **B** or **C**, and put a tick (✔) in the appropriate box.

You will hear each recording twice.

You will hear a man talking about a tennis match he played.

Question 9

How did the man feel during the match?

A   worried he had hurt himself ☐

B   surprised by the other player's attitude ☐

C   annoyed by the delays ☐ [1]

Question 10

What does the man want to do to improve his tennis?

A   watch more professional matches ☐

B   play more matches during the week ☐

C   find a good coach ☐ [1]

Audio for the listening exercises is available in the digital resource.

You will hear a girl talking about a family trip to a town.

Question 11

What was the girl's first impression of the town?

A   There was little for tourists to see. ☐

B   It looked as if little had changed in hundreds of years. ☐

C   The local people were very welcoming. ☐   [1]

Question 12

What did the family do in the town at the end of the day?

A   They departed at the time they'd planned. ☐

B   They enjoyed a special meal. ☐

C   They discovered a beautiful area. ☐   [1]

You will hear a boy talking about the visit of a famous writer to his school.

Question 13

The boy thought that

A   the writer was rather shy. ☐

B   the writer seemed a bit bored. ☐

C   the writer did not behave like a big star. ☐   [1]

Question 14

What advice did the writer give to students who wanted to write a book?

A   be prepared to wait for success ☐

B   do not worry about being original ☐

C   never be afraid of criticism ☐   [1]

Audio for the listening exercises is available in the digital resource.

You will hear a man talking about camping with some friends.

Question 15

What was the man most worried about before going camping?

A   being far away from a town

B   dealing with practical issues

C   the conditions he might face   [1]

Question 16

What was the most positive aspect of the man's experience?

A   he got to know his friends better

B   he stopped thinking about work

C   he learned about the natural world   [1]

You will hear a young woman talking about her first role in a TV drama.

Question 17

What did the woman find surprising when she started to work on the show?

A   how hard her colleagues worked

B   how difficult it was to remember the script

C   how much attention she got from the media   [1]

Question 18

What does the woman say about the fans she met?

A   They asked about things she could not tell them.

B   They had a good sense of humour.

C   They were not afraid to criticise the show.   [1]

[Total: 10]

Audio for the listening exercises is available in the digital resource.

Exercise 3

You will hear a man called Eddie Granger talking about butterflies. For each question, choose the correct answer, **A**, **B** or **C**, and put a tick (✔) in the appropriate box.

You will hear the talk twice.

Now look at questions **19–26**.

Butterflies

Question 19

There are about … species of butterfly in Europe.

A 750 ☐

B 500 ☐

C 260 ☐ [1]

Question 20

Eddie says that most people do not know that butterflies

A taste with their feet. ☐

B have very good vision. ☐

C can travel huge distances. ☐ [1]

Audio for the listening exercises is available in the digital resource.

Question 21

Eddie believes that … is the major reason why butterflies are endangered.

A pollution ☐

B climate change ☐

C habitat loss ☐ [1]

Question 22

Eddie says that he … in order to attract butterflies to his garden.

A puts down some flat stones ☐

B creates pools of water ☐

C leaves fallen fruit on the ground ☐ [1]

Question 23

Eddie says that he was surprised how many … butterflies he has seen in his local area.

A red admiral ☐

B orange tip ☐

C cabbage white ☐ [1]

Question 24

In butterfly centres, the most difficult thing is to make sure the … is right.

A temperature ☐

B humidity ☐

C lighting ☐ [1]

Audio for the listening exercises is available in the digital resource.

Question 25

Eddie did not expect to see … in the butterfly centre he visited.

A passion flowers

B mango trees

C banana plants   [1]

Question 26

The staff member at the butterfly centre told Eddie that her main responsibility is to

A examine the butterflies.

B feed the butterflies.

C water the plants.   [1]

[Total: 8]

Audio for the listening exercises is available in the digital resource.

Exercise 4

 You will hear six people talking about their experiences of learning about history.

For questions **27–32**, choose from the list (**A–H**) showing which idea each speaker expresses. Write the correct letter (**A–H**) on the answer line. Use each letter only once. There are two extra letters which you do not need to use.

You will hear the recordings twice.

Now read statements **A–H**.

| A | I had to make a lot of effort, but it was worth it. |

| B | I appreciated how history helps us understand the present. |

| C | I realised I needed to study the subject in more detail. |

| D | It was difficult for me to imagine life in the past. |

| E | I found all the dates rather boring. |

| F | I understood how history is connected to other subjects. |

| G | I found some explanations confusing. |

| H | I discovered that ancient history is more interesting than other periods. |

Question 27 Speaker 1 .... [1]
Question 28 Speaker 2 .... [1]
Question 29 Speaker 3 .... [1]
Question 30 Speaker 4 .... [1]
Question 31 Speaker 5 .... [1]
Question 32 Speaker 6 .... [1]

[Total: 6]

Audio for the listening exercises is available in the digital resource.

Exercise 5

You will hear an interview with a woman called Rachel Smith, who is a sailor. For each question, choose the correct answer, **A, B** or **C**, and put a tick (✔) in the appropriate box.

You will hear the interview twice.

Now look at questions **33–40**.

Question 33

When Rachel first went to a sailing club, she

A was surprised by what she learnt from the talk.

B was embarrassed about making a mistake.

C had to pretend to enjoy the sailing experience. [1]

Question 34

What does Rachel say about the first time she was at sea for several days?

A She spent a lot of time on boring routine tasks.

B She worried about the crew's attitude to her.

C She was given a chance to take on big challenges. [1]

Question 35

According to Rachel, sailing in a small boat

A meant she put herself in some danger.

B taught her things that were useful later on.

C annoyed her because it was not well equipped. [1]

Question 36

Rachel says that an ideal crew member would be someone who is

A able to deal with difficult situations calmly.

B willing to do the necessary training with her.

C friendly and can see the funny side of things. [1]

Audio for the listening exercises is available in the digital resource.

Question 37

What did Rachel find most difficult about the first race she took part in?

A the lack of time she had to get ready ☐

B the quality of the opposition she faced ☐

C the terrible weather conditions ☐ [1]

Question 38

Rachel says that at the beginning most of her competitors

A said things that affected her confidence. ☐

B found it hard to believe she was doing so well. ☐

C were sometimes willing to give a limited amount of help. ☐ [1]

Question 39

When Rachel is on a long sailing trip, she

A is in constant contact with home. ☐

B finds it difficult to spend time by herself. ☐

C has so much to do there is not time to feel sad. ☐ [1]

Question 40

Rachel thinks winning the race across the Atlantic was special because

A she had been unable to get much rest. ☐

B she had not been concentrating at important moments. ☐

C she had to use equipment that did not work properly. ☐ [1]

[Total: 8]

Audio for the listening exercises is available in the digital resource.

Examiner copy: Practice Test 2 – Speaking

Warm-up (1–2 minutes)

Put the student at ease by conducting a short conversation using the following questions:

- What type of stories do you enjoy reading?
- Where do you usually do your homework?
- How did you meet your best friend?

Part 1 – Interview (2–3 minutes)

Tell the student the topic for this part (sports and games). Conduct a short interview with the student by asking the following questions. If the student does not know how to answer the question, ask the question again. If the student still does not know what to say, move on to the next question.

Sports and games
- What sports and games do people enjoy playing in your country?
- Can you tell me about a time you won a game or a team sport, and what happened?
- Do you think sportspeople make good role models for young people? Why? Why not?

Part 2 – Short talk (3–4 minutes including 1 minute preparation time)

Ask the student to look at their card which contains the following speaking assessment information. The student has up to 1 minute to read the card and prepare for the talk. The student cannot make any written notes. After one minute, ask the student to start their short talk.

A day off

You are planning how to spend your day off. You are considering the following options:

- going to the beach with your friends
- having a picnic with your family.

Discuss the advantages and disadvantages of each option. Say which option you would prefer, and why.

Part 3 – Discussion (3–4 minutes)

Conduct a discussion using the following questions. If the student says very little, encourage a further discussion by asking questions like, *Why do you think so?, Can you tell me a bit more about …?*, etc. If the student does not know what to say, give them a few seconds, then move on to the next question.

- Do you think that for young people it is more important to spend their free time with their friends rather than their family?
- There is an opinion that people need to spend more of their free time outdoors. Would you agree?
- Many people say that in big cities there are not enough things for young people to do in their free time. Do you think this is true?
- The best way to stop people dropping litter in public places is to fine them a lot of money. What is your opinion?

Student copy: Practice Test 2 – Speaking

IMPORTANT: Do not look at this card until the examiner tells you to.

Speaking assessment card

A day off

You are planning how to spend your day off. You are considering the following options:

- going to the beach with your friends
- having a picnic with your family.

Discuss the advantages and disadvantages of each option. Say which option you would prefer, and why.

BLANK PAGE

# Practice Test 3

Reading and Writing

Exercise 1

Read the article about a trip to see wild gorillas in the Volcanoes National Park, in Rwanda in Africa, and then answer the questions.

GORILLA TREKKING

Earlier this year, while on a short holiday in Rwanda in Africa, I saw some wild mountain gorillas in their natural environment. Gorilla trekking – going on long, tough walks to see the animals – is a significant tourist activity in the Virunga Mountains, which extend across both Rwanda and Uganda. The treks offered in the Volcanoes National Park of Rwanda tend to be shorter than those in Uganda's National Park, which is why that option suited me.

Gorilla trekking is a year-round activity, though during the 'long rains' of April and May, conditions are very wet and hiking is at its toughest. The peak season for visitors in July and August is followed by a second rainy season from September to November. The fact is, however, that it can rain at any time, which is why visitors should always have waterproof bags to keep their things dry.

All treks in the park have to be supervised by park rangers who guide visitors to one of several gorilla groups. The rule is there, above all, to protect the gorillas, but, also, most visitors wouldn't be able to do much without guides. Gorillas are good at hiding and the mountain slopes are challenging; the vegetation is so dense and rough that trekkers are advised to bring gardening gloves to protect their hands, and long-sleeved tops to stop their arms getting badly scratched.

Each group of visitors goes in search of one particular gorilla family, called a troop, and the trek, including one hour with the troop, may take anything between three and nine hours. My group hiked for over four hours through thick vegetation along steep, slippery paths. I appreciated my strong walking boots, a must for anyone trekking in the area. Our guides told us there were 19 gorilla troops in the park, with 10–30 individuals in each one. There are thought to be about 500 wild gorillas in the region, almost double the number estimated in 1981, when conservation efforts began to have an effect. Mountain gorillas live at altitudes between 2500 and 4000 metres, and to help them deal with the cold temperatures, they have longer fur than gorillas living at lower altitudes elsewhere in Africa, our guide explained.

When we finally found our gorilla troop, it consisted of two older males, several mothers, younger males and females and at least two babies. Some were sleeping, some were eating leaves and some of the younger ones were playing with each other. Being able to observe these extraordinary creatures close up was an enormous privilege.

Question 1

Why did the writer choose to see the gorillas in Rwanda rather than in Uganda?

.... [1]

Question 2

Which are the busiest months of the year for gorilla trekking?

.... [1]

Question 3

What is the main reason that visitors are supervised in the Volcanoes National Park?

.... [1]

Question 4

How long do visitors spend near the gorillas?

.... [1]

Question 5

How are mountain gorillas physically different from lowland gorillas?

.... [1]

Question 6

What things are visitors recommended to take with them? Give **three** details.

....

....

.... [3]

[Total: 8]

Exercise 2

Read extracts from a magazine article in which four students (**A–D**) write about studying drama at university. Then answer Question **7(a)–(i)**.

DRAMA STUDIES

A   Isabel Monteiro

When I tell people I'm studying drama at university, they often say things like, 'It's all about acting, so how can you study it?', or 'Sounds like three years of having fun'. The fact is, though, my course is seriously hard work. We work on our acting, singing, directing and stage management skills, but we also do research, essays and exams, like any other students. We work a lot in teams, and as most jobs in theatre, film-making and television involve working with other people, this makes sense. In fact, teamworking skills are useful for all sorts of jobs unrelated to drama. Because we spend so much time together – not only studying, but living and socialising too – we become very close friends. Other students notice this, and I've heard them describe us as a little strange and hard to understand. This may have something to do with us all being rather loud and outgoing, but you'd expect that in people attracted to performing.

B   Femi Mensah

I originally went to university to study literature, but I soon realised that a course which included physical activity, performance and creativity, as well as reading and writing, would suit me better. So, I switched to drama studies, and I've never regretted it. This year we did a brilliant project which involved forming a small-scale theatre company and writing, producing and performing a play. This kind of project requires lots of teamwork, but you're allowed lots of freedom to choose how you do things. This does mean you have to be well organised and strict about managing your time, and I've learnt a lot from working like this. My teachers have told me, and I know they're right, that I'm not a naturally talented performer, so I may not end up working in the theatre. The truth is, however, that graduates from my course have become teachers, marketing professionals or even police officers.

C   Natalya Vasiliev

One thing I hadn't realised before I started my drama course was how much theatre and film work relies on a willingness to cooperate. You might be putting on a play in a wonderful theatre with very advanced lighting and sound equipment, as I'm fortunate to be able to do in my university, but you can't avoid working with people who have very different attitudes and approaches. You have to learn to deal with it. As far as I'm concerned, that's a key part of being a drama student. In fact, I'll probably never work in an environment where no-one complains to me and everyone always gets on well, whatever field of work I eventually find myself in. Playwriting is one of the many skills I've been able to develop on my course, and I'd actually like to write plays for a living. If this is not possible, I'll have to look into other jobs I could do.

D Takashi Kimura

I'm in the final year of my drama course and I'm thinking about what I should do next. I'd like to be a theatre actor, though I would be able to do backstage jobs like managing the lighting or the sound because of the different areas we've covered on the course. Finding work is often challenging for young actors. One of the benefits of studying drama here is that we meet people from the worlds of theatre, film and television, and I've even done work experience at one of the top theatres in the city. I've tried to stay in touch with people I've met because they might be able to help me in the future. Everyone says you need to be strong to survive as an actor, and I feel I've become tougher through the projects and performances we've done. This is also thanks to our teachers, who always point out when you've done something wrong or below standard, and you learn to cope with feedback like that.

For each statement, write the correct letter A, B, C or D on the line.

Question 7

Which student mentions the following?

(a) the value of developing a network of contacts .... [1]

(b) the appeal of high-quality facilities .... [1]

(c) a characteristic that many drama students share .... [1]

(d) satisfaction with the balance between academic and practical work .... [1]

(e) a difficult aspect of doing lots of group work .... [1]

(f) a common misunderstanding about drama studies .... [1]

(g) the importance of being able to handle criticism .... [1]

(h) the value of self-discipline .... [1]

(i) the relationships that drama students develop .... [1]

[Total: 9]

Exercise 3

Read the article about a man called Greg Preston, who teaches people how to surf, and then complete the notes.

GREG PRESTON – THE MAN WITH THE DREAM JOB?

For many people it sounds like a dream job. Twenty-eight-year-old Greg Preston teaches people how to surf on Seven Mile Beach in south-east Australia from September to April. Then, from May to August, he goes overseas to teach surfing in places like Indonesia, France, Sri Lanka and South Africa.

'My work gives me the chance to travel, which I love,' he says. 'I'm very lucky really because I love my job too. I'm passionate about surfing. In fact, I don't think you can teach it if you're not.'

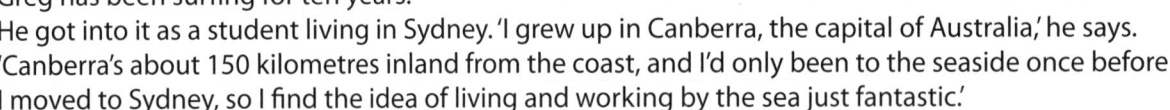

Greg has been surfing for ten years. He got into it as a student living in Sydney. 'I grew up in Canberra, the capital of Australia,' he says. 'Canberra's about 150 kilometres inland from the coast, and I'd only been to the seaside once before I moved to Sydney, so I find the idea of living and working by the sea just fantastic.'

Greg admits that not everything about the job is ideal. 'You have to keep an eye on the learners all the time, which I don't mind too much by the way, but it means you don't have much time to surf yourself. That's frustrating sometimes. But no job's perfect.'

Three years after he started surfing, Greg reached an advanced level and trained to become a qualified instructor. 'You don't have to be qualified to be able to teach surfing,' Greg says. 'But it's essential to be very aware of safety, and the instructor courses are helpful for that.'

As in many sports, there are risks involved in surfing. Something that Greg never looks forward to is telling students that they can't go into the water. 'The sea is too dangerous sometimes,' he says, 'but people get very disappointed when they can't have lessons. I don't know why they find it so hard to accept. You just have to explain the situation to them. They get their money back if there are no classes, of course. But I don't think you can do the job properly unless you're a good communicator.'

Greg gets asked lots of questions about surfing and about his job. His students come from many different backgrounds. His current class includes two college students, a Japanese tourist, two builders and an artist. But the same questions are asked again and again, like 'What's the biggest wave you've ever ridden?' and 'Is part of your job fixing the surfboards when they get damaged?', to which Greg replies 'Yes, and it puts me in a bad mood'. Other common questions are 'Do you ever see sharks?' and 'Do you have to be very fit to teach surfing?' The answer to the last question is 'absolutely,' Greg says. He doesn't mind answering the questions, even though they can be repetitive. It actually helps him build up a relationship with the people he's teaching. And seeing students manage to ride a wave is really satisfying, he says, even though they're only with him for a few lessons.

Imagine you are going to give a talk about the work of a surf instructor to your class at school.

Use words from the article to help you write some notes.

Make short notes under each heading.

Question 8

What Greg likes about being a surf instructor:

Example: *the chance to travel*

- ....
- .... [2]

Question 9

What Greg dislikes about being a surf instructor:

- ....
- .... [2]

Question 10

What Greg believes a surf instructor needs to be:

- ....
- ....
- .... [3]

[Total: 7]

Exercise 4

Read the article written by a wildlife photographer, and then answer the questions.

Photography World's 'Article of the month'

submitted by photographer Marina Patterson

I started taking photos of animals when I was young, and I've just never stopped. Travel has also always been a passion of mine, and photography seemed like a potential way of making a living whilst still being able to experience other countries. For a few years, I had a full-time job in sales to earn enough money to support me, and I focused on photography during my holidays. I worked on improving my skills during this time, and even started my own photography website. A couple of years ago, after long discussions with my friends, including some who were themselves very successful in the photography industry, it felt like the right time to resign from my sales position and become a full-time photographer!

Of course, photography has its challenges, like any job. It's a very competitive industry, and making sure your work stands out, by coming up with new approaches, is really tricky. What you'll also discover is that when you're working with animals, you must be prepared to devote time and effort into studying different species; to becoming something of an expert in whatever you're planning to photograph, in fact. If you're interested in wildlife, like me, this isn't something you'll mind though! You'll also require lots of patience. Anyone who knows me would think I'd struggle with this – I'm known for being constantly active. But they'd be wrong, as I appreciate the stillness and calm I find in the minutes – or sometimes hours – it takes to get the perfect photo.

My last trip was to a wildlife reserve in Kenya, where, together with a couple of photographer friends, I stayed for just over a month. I was hoping to take pictures of the 'big five' – lions, leopards, black rhinos, elephants and African buffalo – for an international wildlife magazine. **They** had provided very specific instructions as to what was required. With wild animals, though, you can never guarantee what will appear each day. That's the case even if you're based in an excellent nature reserve, such as the place where I was staying. But going for that length of time meant I was pretty confident I'd greatly increase my chances of getting what I needed. I also knew I could recover the cost of my extended stay through the extra pictures I was able to take whilst there. I'd been to that nature reserve before, and had remembered it as being an isolated, rather quiet place. I certainly hadn't realised it'd become such a popular tourist destination. This was positive news for local businesses, but for me it meant having to hire a private guide to go to locations off the main routes, giving me the space and conditions I required to work in peace.

My photography has taken me all over the world, but conservation is a common theme throughout my projects. It's vital that work being done to protect wildlife from a range of dangerous threats is recognised. Wherever possible, I visit nature reserves run by conservationists, many of whom work for a small salary, or even for free. By doing so, I know my entrance fee is going to a good cause. But above all, I realise that people aren't typically going to care much about something they have no idea about. My pictures show what's happening to species in different parts of the world, and help highlight the need for action. It's a job I love doing, with each new assignment bringing new opportunities and adventures.

Question 11

In paragraph 1, Marina describes

A   the cost of becoming a photographer. ☐

B   a way of making good professional contacts. ☐

C   some preparations for turning an interest into a job. ☐   [1]

Question 12

What does Marina say she finds hard about her current job?

A   obtaining the right qualifications ☐

B   creating photographs that are unique ☐

C   waiting a long time for the animals to arrive ☐   [1]

Question 13

What does 'they' refer to in line 19?

A   the people Marina was working for at the time ☐

B   the staff at the wildlife reserve where Marina stayed ☐

C   the companions Marina travelled to Kenya with ☐   [1]

Question 14

When Marina was working in Kenya, she was

A   aware she might not make much money from the trip. ☐

B   concerned she wouldn't find the animals she needed. ☐

C   surprised by the numbers of visitors in the area. ☐   [1]

Question 15

In the last paragraph, we learn that Marina supports conservation work by

A   volunteering on various projects.

B   educating the public about issues.

C   raising money for endangered species. [1]

Question 16

This article describes

A   the changing responsibilities of a particular job.

B   the challenges of photographing wild animals.

C   the life of someone who has achieved an ambition. [1]

Exercise 5
Question 17

One of your teachers recently gave you some advice about a problem that you had.

Write an email to a friend explaining what happened.

In your email, you should:

- describe the problem that you had
- explain the advice that the teacher gave you
- say whether the advice has been useful and why.

Write about 120 to 160 words.

You will receive up to 6 marks for the content of your email, and up to 9 marks for the language used.

[Total: 15]

Exercise 6

Question 18

An international student magazine wants to publish some articles about different festivals around the world. You decide to write an article about a festival in your country that you think young people in other countries would find interesting.

In your article, describe what happens in the festival and explain why you think the festival is important for people in your country.

Here are some comments from other students in your class:

> *It brings people together.*

> *It's very different from what people do the rest of the year.*

> *Some people want to change what happens at the festival.*

> *It takes a long time to get everything ready!*

Write the article for the magazine.

The comments above may give you some ideas, and you should also use some ideas of your own.

Write about 120 to 160 words.

You will receive up to 6 marks for the content of your article, and up to 9 marks for the language used.

[Total: 15]

Practice Test 3
Listening

Exercise 1

 You will hear eight short recordings. For each question, choose the correct answer, **A**, **B**, **C** or **D**, and put a tick (✔) in the appropriate box.

You will hear each recording twice.

Question 1

What did the woman do in town today?

A ☐ B ☐ C ☐ D ☐ [1]

Question 2

What is the boy reading about?

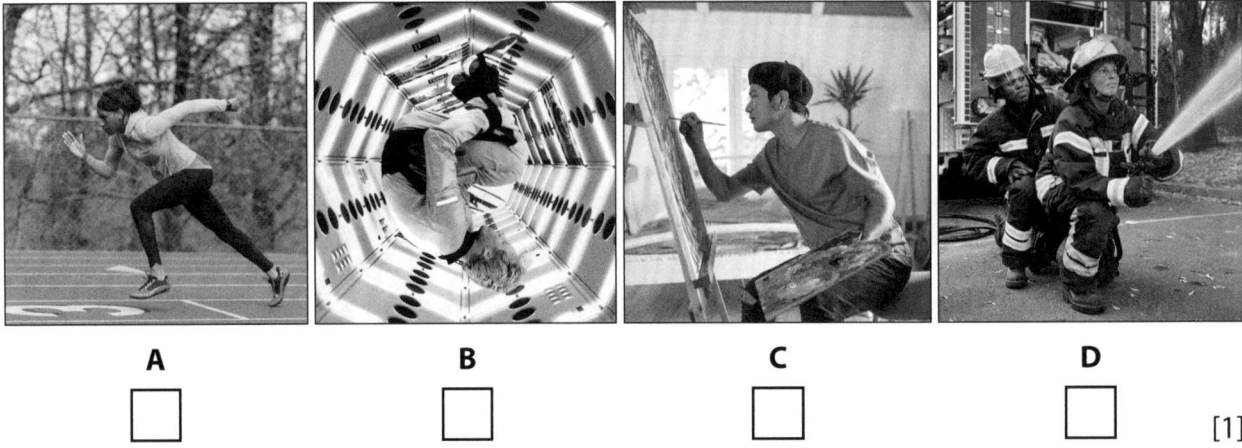

A ☐ B ☐ C ☐ D ☐ [1]

Audio for the listening exercises is available in the digital resource.

Question 3

What change does the woman want to make to her garden?

A ☐ B ☐ C ☐ D ☐ [1]

Question 4

What event did the boy attend?

A ☐ B ☐ C ☐ D ☐ [1]

Audio for the listening exercises is available in the digital resource.

Question 5

Why was the boy unable to go to his friend's party?

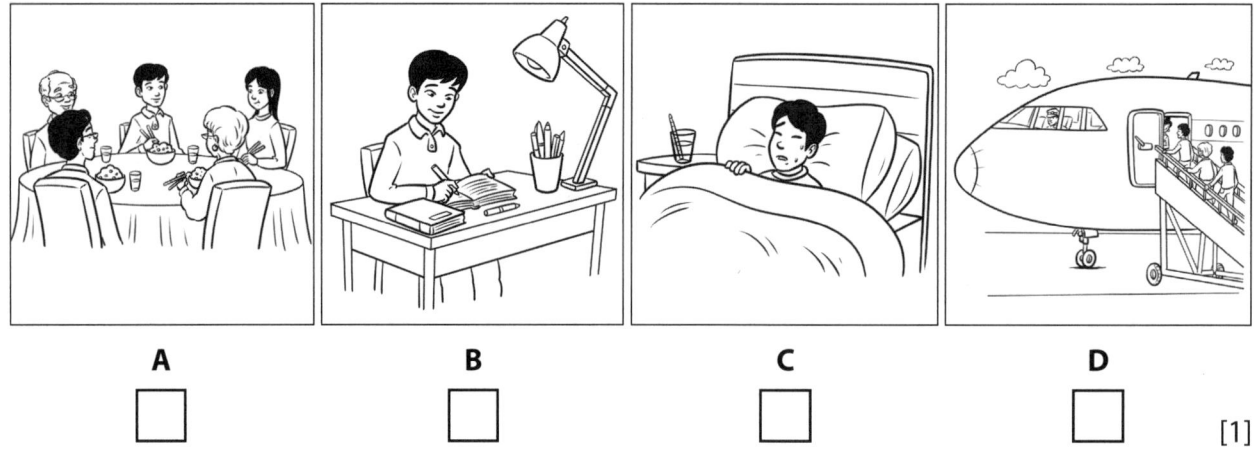

A ☐ B ☐ C ☐ D ☐ [1]

Question 6

What did the girl lose on the coach?

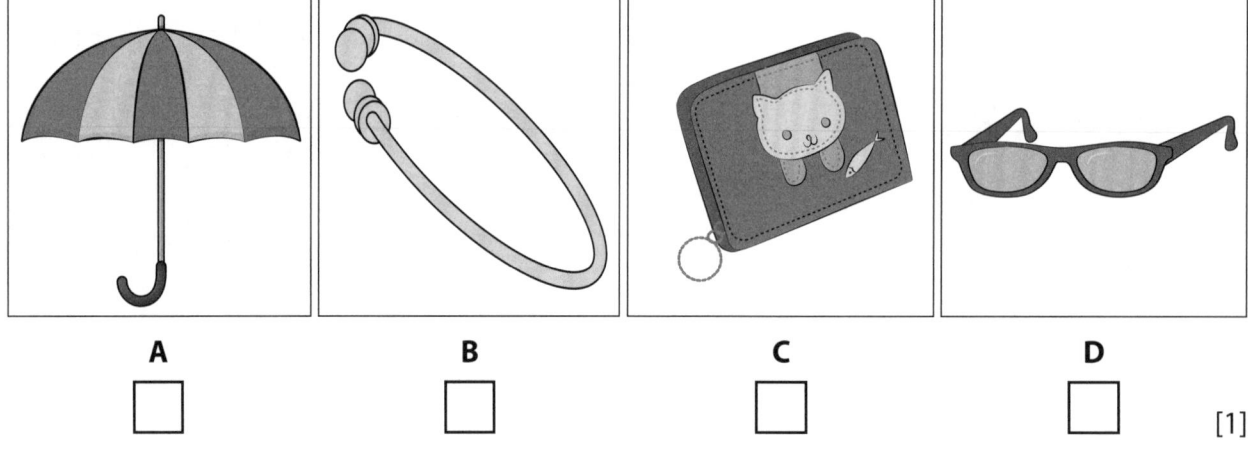

A ☐ B ☐ C ☐ D ☐ [1]

Audio for the listening exercises is available in the digital resource.

Question 7

How will the girl relax this weekend?

A ☐ B ☐ C ☐ D ☐ [1]

Question 8

Why was the man late for his meeting?

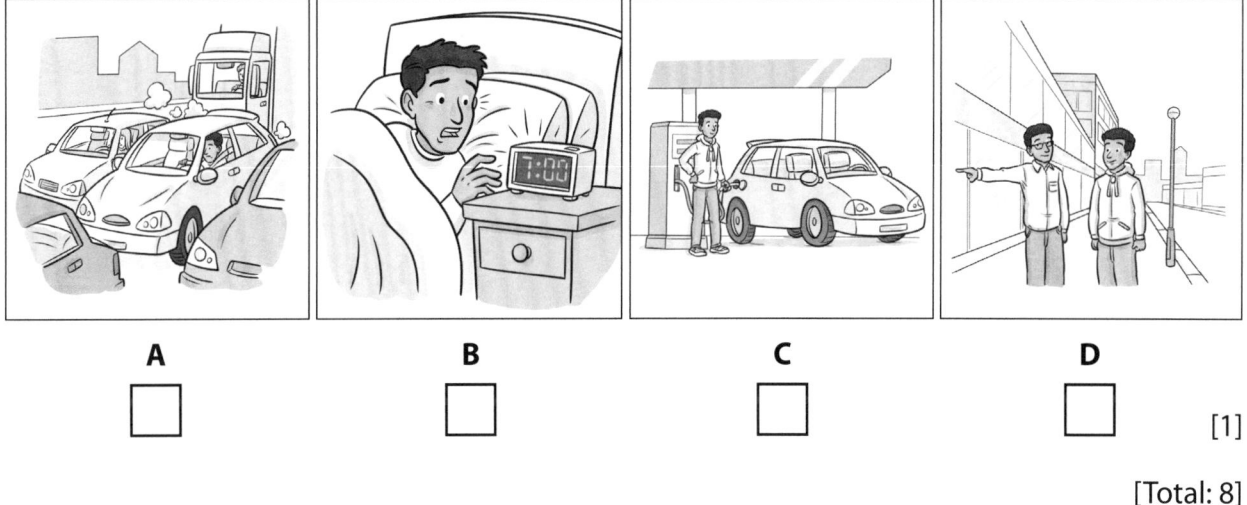

A ☐ B ☐ C ☐ D ☐ [1]

[Total: 8]

Audio for the listening exercises is available in the digital resource.

Exercise 2

 You will hear five short recordings. For each question, choose the correct answer, **A**, **B** or **C**, and put a tick (✔) in the appropriate box.

You will hear each recording twice.

You will hear a girl talking about a fashion show.

Question 9

What problem did the organisers have when planning the show?

A not having enough money

B deciding on a theme

C finding a suitable location [1]

Question 10

The girl thinks the show was successful because of

A the very effective advertising.

B the low entrance fee.

C the talent of the students taking part. [1]

Audio for the listening exercises is available in the digital resource.

You will hear two friends talking about a football match.

Question 11

What impressed the friends most about the football match?

A   the way the team dealt with difficult situations ☐

B   the referee's ability to keep people calm ☐

C   the decisions made by the manager ☐   [1]

Question 12

What does the girl think about the captain of the team?

A   He helped other players to be more confident. ☐

B   He was clearly the best player on the day. ☐

C   He showed that he was very responsible. ☐   [1]

You will hear a recorded message about a photography course at a college.

Question 13

In the message, the speaker says that

A   students need to have good cameras. ☐

B   it is more convenient to book online. ☐

C   the course is suitable for complete beginners. ☐   [1]

Question 14

What is special about the course this year?

A   One of the tutors is quite famous. ☐

B   The lessons will be outdoors. ☐

C   The fees have been reduced. ☐   [1]

Audio for the listening exercises is available in the digital resource.

You will hear a woman talking about her recent trip.

Question 15

How did the woman feel about the trip before leaving?

A   annoyed she had not done some research

B   nervous about the route she would have to take

C   disappointed it was not a suitable day for the visit   [1]

Question 16

What did the woman enjoy most about the trip?

A   the feeling of freedom

B   the chance to have a rest

C   the nice surprise she had   [1]

You will hear a man giving a review of a new cartoon.

Question 17

Where does the cartoon begin?

A   on a ship

B   in a kitchen

C   on a mountain top   [1]

Question 18

Why does he think the film will be popular?

A   It has interesting characters.

B   It has an amusing script.

C   It has an imaginative plot.   [1]

[Total: 10]

Audio for the listening exercises is available in the digital resource.

Exercise 3

 You will hear a man called Oliver Connors talking about his work as an oceanographer, someone who studies the sea. For each question, choose the correct answer, **A**, **B** or **C**, and put a tick (✔) in the appropriate box.

You will hear the talk twice.

Now look at questions **19–26**.

Exploring the oceans

Question 19

Oliver started his career as an oceanographer doing research on … in the sea.

A the rocks ☐

B the plants ☐

C the animals ☐   [1]

Audio for the listening exercises is available in the digital resource.

Question 20

Oliver's most recent project involved helping to investigate

A a shipwreck.

B ocean currents and waves.

C an underwater volcano. [1]

Question 21

Oliver's current work involves looking for new species using

A a team of divers.

B a submarine.

C a robotic vehicle. [1]

Question 22

When thinking about the future health of the oceans, Oliver's greatest worry is

A oil spills.

B plastic pollution.

C the amount of acid in the water. [1]

Question 23

Oliver says that the place called the Mariana Trench is … kilometres deep.

A 3.5

B 7

C 11 [1]

Audio for the listening exercises is available in the digital resource.

Question 24

Oliver says that the … at the bottom of the Mariana Trench is the most surprising thing about the place.

A   darkness

B   temperature

C   pressure [1]

Question 25

Oliver says that one of the most fascinating sea creatures is the

A   dolphin.

B   turtle.

C   octopus. [1]

Question 26

Oliver has decided to join a campaign to

A   stop some species dying out.

B   create more marine reserves.

C   reduce the amount of fishing. [1]

[Total: 8]

Audio for the listening exercises is available in the digital resource.

Exercise 4

You will hear six people talking about meals they have had.

For questions **27–32**, choose from the list (**A–H**) showing which idea each speaker expresses. Write the correct letter (**A–H**) on the answer line. Use each letter only once. There are two extra letters which you do not need to use.

You will hear the recordings twice.

Now read statements **A–H**.

| **A** | The variety of food was great. |

| **B** | It was not planned very carefully. |

| **C** | The location made the occasion special. |

| **D** | It was an opportunity to meet new people. |

| **E** | The atmosphere changed quite quickly. |

| **F** | The number of people caused problems. |

| **G** | It was more fun than I expected. |

| **H** | The food has inspired me to cook more. |

Question 27	Speaker 1	[1]
Question 28	Speaker 2	[1]
Question 29	Speaker 3	[1]
Question 30	Speaker 4	[1]
Question 31	Speaker 5	[1]
Question 32	Speaker 6	[1]

[Total: 6]

Audio for the listening exercises is available in the digital resource.

Exercise 5

 You will hear an interview with a woman called Isabelle Navarro, who manages rock bands. For each question, choose the correct answer, **A**, **B** or **C**, and put a tick (✔) in the appropriate box.

You will hear the interview twice.

Now look at questions **33–40**.

Question 33

Isabelle Navarro works with people who have

A shown some ability to organise themselves. ☐

B already managed to achieve something locally. ☐

C a strong belief in their ability to do well. ☐   [1]

Question 34

Isabelle says that she decided to manage her first band because

A she believed it would not be very difficult to do. ☐

B she was inspired by a book about famous managers. ☐

C she realised she could never be a singer herself. ☐   [1]

Question 35

How did Isabelle feel when her first band had a hit record?

A unsure that she had played an important role. ☐

B worried the success would not be repeated. ☐

C surprised by the attention she received. ☐   [1]

Question 36

Isabelle says her advice to new rock bands would be to

A try to record their first album as soon as they can. ☐

B discuss with other musicians what they should do. ☐

C have the courage to ignore the latest fashion in music. ☐   [1]

Audio for the listening exercises is available in the digital resource.

Question 37

What does she say about her relationship with the band called the Big Cats?

A It was sometimes necessary to annoy the band members.

B It lasted much longer than she expected it to.

C It took a while for both sides to trust one another. [1]

Question 38

Isabelle usually manages only soft rock bands because

A she has a reputation for success with such musicians.

B she has loved that type of music all her life.

C she has limited knowledge of other types of music. [1]

Question 39

Isabelle believes that a successful manager of a rock band needs to

A be willing to work very long hours.

B react to constant problems seriously.

C be able to take on many completely different roles. [1]

Question 40

How does Isabelle think that the music business has changed in recent years?

A Bands ask for their fans' opinions about what they should do.

B Bands expect to become successful very quickly.

C Bands are less likely to work with a manager. [1]

[Total: 8]

Audio for the listening exercises is available in the digital resource.

Examiner copy: Practice Test 3 – Speaking

Warm-up (1–2 minutes)

Put the student at ease by conducting a short conversation using the following questions:

- How far do you live from your school?
- Where did you go on your last holiday?
- How often do you watch films?

Part 1 – Interview (2–3 minutes)

Tell the student the topic for this part (people around us). Conduct a short interview with the student by asking the following questions. If the student does not know how to answer the question, ask the question again. If the student still does not know what to say, move on to the next question.

People around us

- What things can young people learn from their grandparents?
- Can you tell me how you met your best friend?
- Do you think that, in the future, it will become more difficult for us to meet new people face to face? Why? Why not?

Part 2 – Short talk (3–4 minutes including 1 minute preparation time)

Ask the student to look at their card which contains the following speaking assessment information. The student has up to 1 minute to read the card and prepare for the talk. The student cannot make any written notes. After one minute, ask the student to start their short talk.

Competitions

You are planning to enter a competition to represent your school. You are considering the following options:

- a running race
- a spelling competition.

Discuss how easy or difficult it is to prepare for each competition. Say which competition you would prefer to enter, and why.

Part 3 – Discussion (3–4 minutes)

Conduct a discussion using the following questions. If the student says very little, encourage a further discussion by asking questions like, *Why do you think so?, Can you tell me a bit more about …?*, etc. If the student does not know what to say, give them a few seconds, then move on to the next question.

- Many people say that sportspeople who cheat in competitions should not be allowed to represent their country ever again. What is your opinion?
- Why do you think some people do not enjoy running?
- Is money a good prize for winning a school competition? Why? Why not?
- There is an opinion that all competitors need live audiences to perform better. Would you agree?

Student copy: Practice Test 3 – Speaking

IMPORTANT: Do not look at this card until the examiner tells you to.

Speaking assessment card

Competitions

You are planning to enter a competition to respresent your school. You are considering the following options:

- a running race
- a spelling competition.

Discuss how easy or difficult it is prepare for each competition. Say which competition you would prefer to enter, and why.

BLANK PAGE

Practice Test 4

Reading and Writing

Exercise 1

Read the article in which a journalist, called Gavin Stevens, describes how he climbed Aconcagua, a mountain in South America, and then answer the questions.

CLIMBING ACONCAGUA

I had always dreamed of climbing a high mountain. One day, I read about Aconcagua in Argentina. It's 7000 metres high, but you can reach the top without rock-climbing skills so I decided to book a place on a guided climb.

My climbing group consisted of seven people, and was led by three local guides. We set off from the entrance of Aconcagua Provincial Park and hiked for three days across grassland, desert and rocky hills to get to Base Camp. At one point, a sandstorm delayed us for five hours, but the walking built up our strength.

At 4300 metres above sea level, Aconcagua Base Camp, as I'd seen in photos online, is a strange-looking collection of colourful tents, washing facilities, a helicopter pad and a volleyball court. There was also a plastic palm tree, which seemed completely out of place to me.

We stayed there for four days to get used to the altitude. With low oxygen levels, sleeping is hard and you feel breathless and dizzy, so we rested and chatted to other climbers. Before we moved up to Camp 1, where we spent two nights, one of our team was forced to drop out because of a chest infection. At that altitude (5000 metres), it's essential to drink lots of water, but it's too heavy to be carrying a lot. The guides solve this problem by collecting snow to melt for tea, and I was happy to give them a hand while others in the group checked the weather forecasts.

On the two nights we spent at Camp 2 (5550 metres), the temperature dropped below minus 30° C and the wind was incredibly strong. To stop it destroying our tents, we built walls of rocks around them, but sleep was almost impossible. After the first night there, a man in our team decided he couldn't go on. He was suffering from severe exhaustion, so a guide accompanied him back to Base Camp.

On the night we spent at Camp 3 (6000 metres), the wind dropped a little, but it snowed. On the last day of the climb, we set off at 5 a.m. Our progress was slow, and at 6300 metres, one of the climbers had no feeling in her feet or hands. The guides said it was too risky for her to continue, and one of them took her down.

That left four of us with one guide. We eventually reached the top after eleven days of sleeplessness, breathlessness and pain. We completed the last stage in nine hours. I'd found it incredibly tough, but for one hour, we stood on the highest place on earth outside the Himalayas. We took photos, ate something, and then it was time to descend, bringing with us memories that will last a lifetime.

Question 1

What made the hike to the Base Camp slower than usual?

.... [1]

Question 2

What was the writer surprised to see at the Base Camp?

.... [1]

Question 3

How did the writer help the guides at Camp 1?

.... [1]

Question 4

How did the climbers protect their tents from the wind?

.... [1]

Question 5

How long did the final section of the climb take?

.... [1]

Question 6

Why did some people from the climbing group have to give up before reaching the top of the mountain? Give **three** reasons.

....

....

.... [3]

[Total: 8]

Exercise 2

Read the reviews of four computer games (**A–D**). Then answer Question **7(a)–(i)**.

REVIEWS OF COMPUTER GAMES

A *Planet Kree*

When Arsenio Vroom lands his damaged spacecraft on the planet Kree, he finds himself in the middle of a battle for control of the distant planet. This reminds me of science fiction games I used to play 15 or 20 years ago, and so does the soundtrack and even the types of tasks you have to deal with as a player. I must admit that I loved all this about it. Generally, younger gamers in particular are likely to enjoy the cartoon-like art and the jokey, often weird communication between the characters, but there may not be as much to keep the interest of a more mature generation of players – apart from the occasional individual like me. The game starts with us following Arsenio, but we soon meet lots of other fantasy characters. In fact, there are so many that you forget who is who, what they have done and what they are trying to do. Apart from this, however, the game is excellent.

B *Motorbike Marvels*

Motorbike fans will love this game, and I can't see why it shouldn't appeal to people who are too young to have ever sat on a motorbike. The bikes look fantastic as they speed around the racetracks, and the game designers have definitely managed to recreate the thrilling atmosphere and the amazing range of colour and movement you get at races. You can play solo or with others online, and you can choose your competitions, riders and bikes. These range from beautiful classic models from 50 or 60 years ago to super-advanced modern machines. It's a pity the difficulty levels are often much too high in the races, and there's nothing you can do to change this. I lost count of the number of times my riders crashed. On the other hand, I loved playing the role of racing team manager. Lots of detailed information is provided about the bikes and each rider – personality, riding style, career records, and so on – and it all seems very realistic.

C *Settlers*

In *Settlers*, players control a group of travellers who settle and establish a new community in an unnamed country. They give the characters traditional roles and tasks. One, for example, becomes a builder who constructs homes and other buildings for the community; another organises entertainment. Some tasks seem much more demanding than others. Basically, it's an update on *Villagers*, which came out about ten years ago. In my view, *Settlers* doesn't have enough new features to make it really satisfying, but it has its strong points – its really likeable characters, for example. But if your preference is for fast-moving, all-action games, then *Settlers* is unlikely to be your first choice. I got much more enjoyment out of playing it with a couple of friends than I did playing it on my own, and I imagine this would be true for most people.

D *Tracks*

Some music games are well-made and popular. *Guitar Hero* and *Rock Band* are two that come to mind, but many don't really work. A lot of them do exactly the same things, and then a few others are too complex for ordinary gamers to cope with. *Tracks* is different. The idea is that a group of friends gather in a recording studio to make a record. Players control the musicians and studio engineers, and eventually create an album of whatever musical style or quality they like. It's a long and tricky process, which I first thought might be rather boring, but actually I found it to be completely the opposite. I loved trying out different sounds and instruments, from classical violins and organs to the latest electronic devices. Creative people often have unusual personalities, and the musicians in this game are no exception. In fact, some are so extreme that they are unbelievable – it would be better if they weren't like that. But I still loved the game.

For each question write the correct letter A, B, C or D on the line.

Question 7

Which reviewer…

(a) thinks the game is too similar to previous versions of it? .... [1]

(b) finds the game surprisingly exciting? .... [1]

(c) suggests that the game would not suit all ages? .... [1]

(d) thinks the story in the game is too complicated? .... [1]

(e) says that some of the challenges in the game are unfair? .... [1]

(f) suggests it is better to play the game with other people? .... [1]

(g) wishes the characters were more natural? .... [1]

(h) appreciates the old-fashioned style of the game? .... [1]

(i) is impressed by the visual effects in the game? .... [1]

[Total: 9]

Exercise 3

Read the article about a professional table tennis player called Arjun Chandran, and then complete the notes.

THE PROFESSIONAL TABLE TENNIS PLAYER

Thirty-two-year-old Arjun Chandran is one of the best table tennis players in India. Three years ago he was among the top 200 players in the world, and he has competed in many countries including the USA, Japan and China. His experiences in China made a big impression on him. 'Chinese players win most of the medals at the major international competitions,' he said. 'When you go to China, though, it doesn't seem that surprising. Far more people play table tennis there than anywhere else in the world.'

Arjun has been a professional player for 12 years, and he believes players are now much fitter than when he started out. He has had to work hard to keep up with his rivals, but it has been worth it.

A small increase in the size of the balls is another fairly recent development. Table tennis as played by professionals is extremely fast, and people watching appreciate the fact that the ball now moves through the air more slowly as a result. But Arjun thinks further changes are needed to make the sport more spectator-friendly. At present, in international competitions, a single ball is used throughout a match, unless it gets damaged and needs replacing. Arjun thinks it would be better to have several balls available for players to use. 'The game would flow better,' he says.

It has been suggested that the net should be higher, but Arjun believes this would only help certain types of players. 'We now have more variety of playing styles than in the past,' he says. 'I'm quite aggressive, but others are defensive or technical – and I think that makes things interesting for people watching.' What he would like, however, is stricter rules about the rubber covers on the players' bats. There are many different ones and they affect the way players hit the ball. Arjun thinks this confuses members of the public.

Two years ago, Arjun set up a children's table tennis academy in India, having seen similar schools in China. 'Kids there start playing table tennis very young – at five or six. All those medals that the Chinese win are partly a result of this. Indian players usually don't start playing until they're 15. It makes a big difference.' Arjun has also seen very advanced training methods in China. He believes they are a key factor in the Chinese success story, and he wants young Indian players in his school to benefit from them.

'One of the great advances in my time as a player has been much better analysis of opponents before matches,' says Arjun. 'I think I can teach young players to do that.' Arjun has not yet retired from international competitions, but his future is clear: to do everything he can to help young Indian table tennis players.

Imagine you are going to give a talk about Arjun Chandran and his views on table tennis to your class at school.

Use words from the article to help you write some notes.

Make short notes under each heading.

Question 8

How professional table tennis has changed during Arjun's career:

Example: *players are (now much) fitter*

- ....

- ....

- .... [3]

Question 9

Reasons why Chinese table tennis players are the best in the world:

- ....

- .... [2]

Question 10

Arjun's ideas for making table tennis more popular with spectators in the future:

- ....

- .... [2]

[Total: 7]

Exercise 4

Read the blog written by someone who has entered a technology competition for young people, and then answer the questions.

'TECHNOLOGY BY TEENS' COMPETITION

by Alex Bridges

Recently, I had the chance to enter a national competition called 'Technology by Teens'. I entered with four others, making a team to represent my school – our science teacher had often put us together before to do projects in class, so we knew we got on well. I'd known about the event for a while, as a team of previous winners had visited our school to share their experiences and encourage people to take part. They told us how all the winners got to be involved with various technology research programmes. We all agreed this sounded incredible.

Our team's first task was choosing our project. The competition rule was just that the design needed an environmental benefit – a wide topic! We'd studied award-winning environmental projects in class, like machines that collect tonnes of pollution from the sea. We were thinking smaller scale; specifically something with a practical daily use. My team came up with a small device that measures chemical changes in the meat and fish products you might store, and a light indicates whether they're safe to eat. We didn't know what we'd be competing against, but we hoped people might at least be interested in our device.

We certainly thought it had potential, especially following a business presentation we watched all about food waste in the food industry. Although it focussed on modern production processes, and in particular the impacts on profits, we could see **this** was an issue in domestic settings too. Most people, understandably, get rid of items that have been in their fridges after a while, rather than risk eating something that's not safe. There is then an environmental impact from buying replacement food: more lorries on the roads and more packaging ending up as rubbish.

Our teachers were supportive, and allocated us a room to work in after school. We also knew they'd be happy to offer suggestions, on the understanding that we made any final decisions. Actually, when we finished, knowing we'd done everything ourselves was extremely satisfying. The rules said that it wasn't essential to have a fully working model. You just needed to demonstrate your idea clearly. I think this was partly so that people weren't restricted by things like cost. We managed to make a device that worked well enough to show the judges. Our presentation and display boards explored the full extent of its potential, but we wanted to have something physical that people could touch, to help them understand the concept.

The competition was held in an exhibition hall. On the day, we got to the hall, set up our display and had a quick walk around to see the other competitors and their projects for the first time. An old assumption was that boys were more interested in science and tech than girls, but just a glance around the hall would prove that it was definitely no longer true! We would have liked the time to chat to the other competitors but we had to prepare to give our presentation to the judges, a task which I'd reluctantly volunteered for. In the end, I surprised myself with how smoothly it went, and I definitely won't be anxious next time I have to do something like that.

Although we didn't win, our idea was highly praised. And who knows – perhaps one day every fridge will have one of our devices. Then we'll really have made a difference!

Question 11

In paragraph 1, we learn that

A   Alex's school had won the competition in previous years. ☐

B   Alex and her classmates were impressed by the competition prizes. ☐

C   Alex asked a teacher to suggest which students would make a good team. ☐   [1]

Question 12

Alex's team chose their particular competition entry because

A   they thought it had a good chance of winning. ☐

B   they had already started working on the design in class. ☐

C   they wanted to create a product that people could use at home. ☐   [1]

Question 13

What does 'this' in line 16 refer to?

A   food waste ☐

B   impacts on profits ☐

C   modern production processes ☐   [1]

Question 14

In paragraph 4, Alex explains that the group

A   produced a simple version of their idea for the judges. ☐

B   benefitted from some advice teachers gave them. ☐

C   were limited by the rules of the competition. ☐   [1]

Question 15

What does Alex say about her experience at the event?

A It allowed her to make useful contacts. ☐

B She noticed it was more popular with one gender. ☐

C Her confidence improved as a result of taking part. ☐ [1]

Question 16

What was Alex's reason for writing this blog?

A to inform readers about an interesting experience ☐

B to recommend readers take advantage of opportunities ☐

C to tell readers about the process of developing new technology ☐ [1]

[Total: 6]

Exercise 5
Question 17

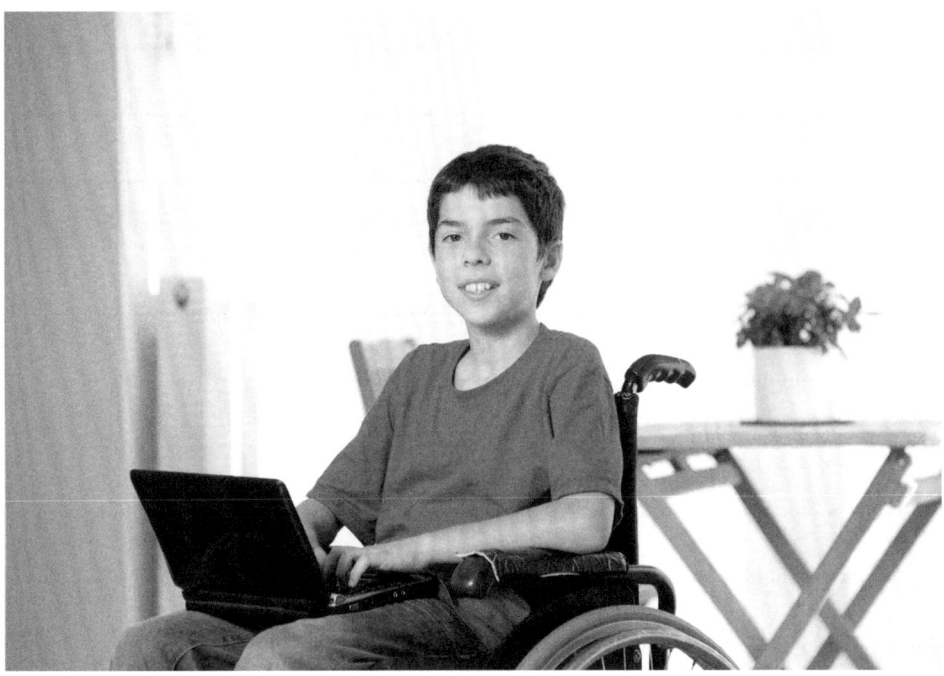

You recently found the email address of an old friend who you have not seen or spoken to for two years.

Write an email to your old friend. In your email, you should:

- ask for some information about your friend's life in the last two years
- explain what your life has been like
- suggest that you and your friend meet up and what you can do.

Write about 120 to 160 words.

You will receive up to 6 marks for the content of your email, and up to 9 marks for the language used.

[Total: 15]

Exercise 6

Question 18

Your class have been talking about entertainment for young people and how important it is for them. Now your teacher has asked you to write an essay for homework.

In your essay, you should write about how important entertainment is for young people.

Here are some comments from students in your class:

Entertainment gives young people a break from study.

Young people like having fun things to do with their friends.

It can be expensive to go to the cinema and concerts.

Young people don't have much free time for entertainment nowadays.

Write your essay for your teacher.

The comments above may give you some ideas, and you should also use some ideas of your own.

Write about 120 to 160 words.

You will receive up to 6 marks for the content of your essay, and up to 9 marks for the language used.

[Total: 15]

Practice Test 4

Listening

Exercise 1

 You will hear eight short recordings. For each question, choose the correct answer, **A**, **B**, **C** or **D**, and put a tick (✔) in the appropriate box.

You will hear each recording twice.

Question 1

What did the woman buy for her best friend's wedding?

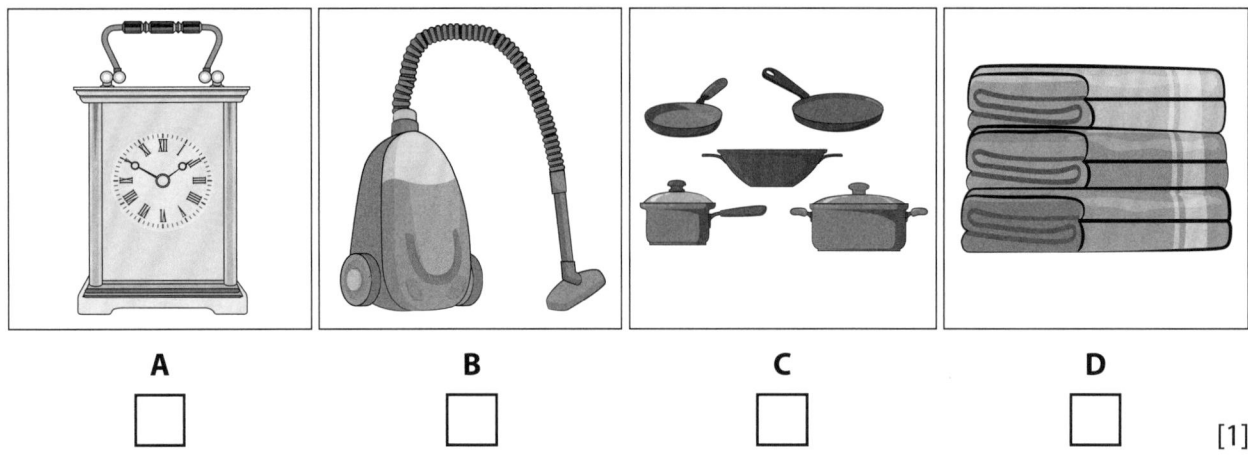

[1]

Question 2

What does the man think he spent too much time doing last weekend?

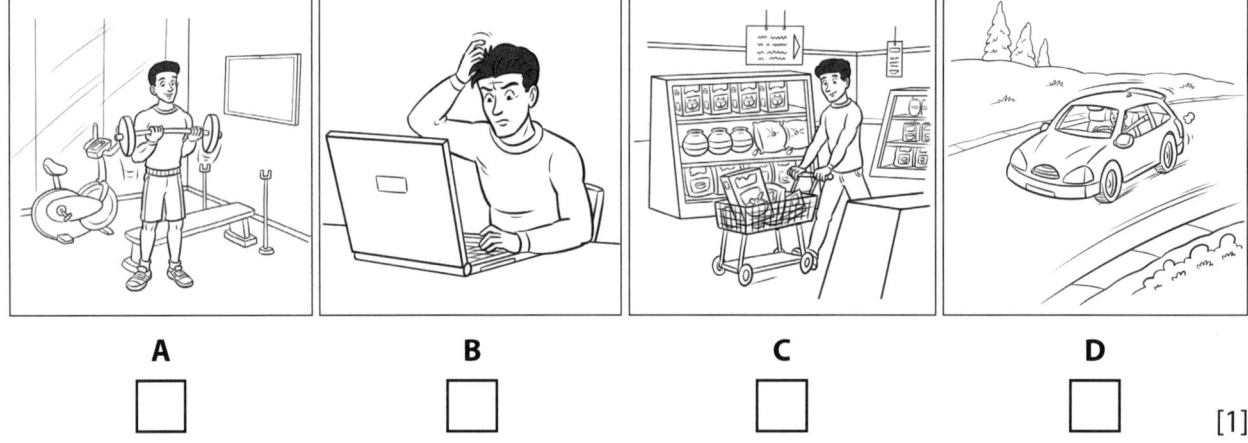

[1]

Audio for the listening exercises is available in the digital resource.

Question 3

What job does the girl's aunt do?

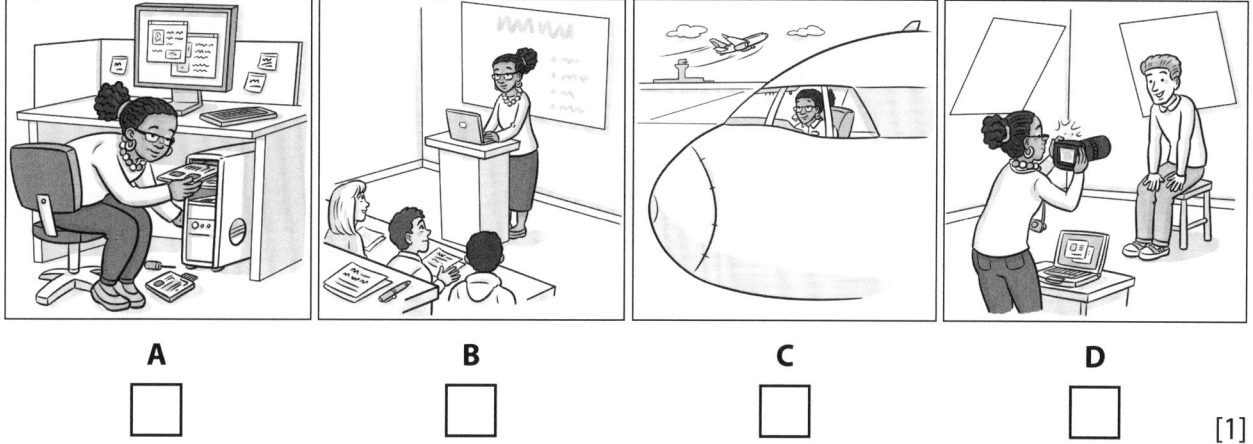

[1]

Question 4

How did the woman travel to her hotel?

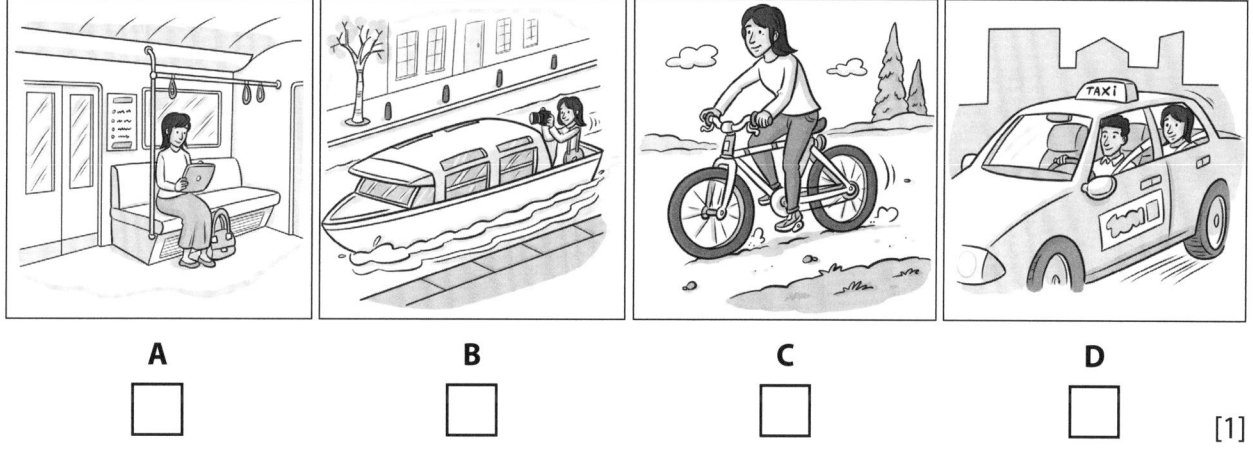

[1]

Audio for the listening exercises is available in the digital resource.

Question 5

What does the man sell at the local market?

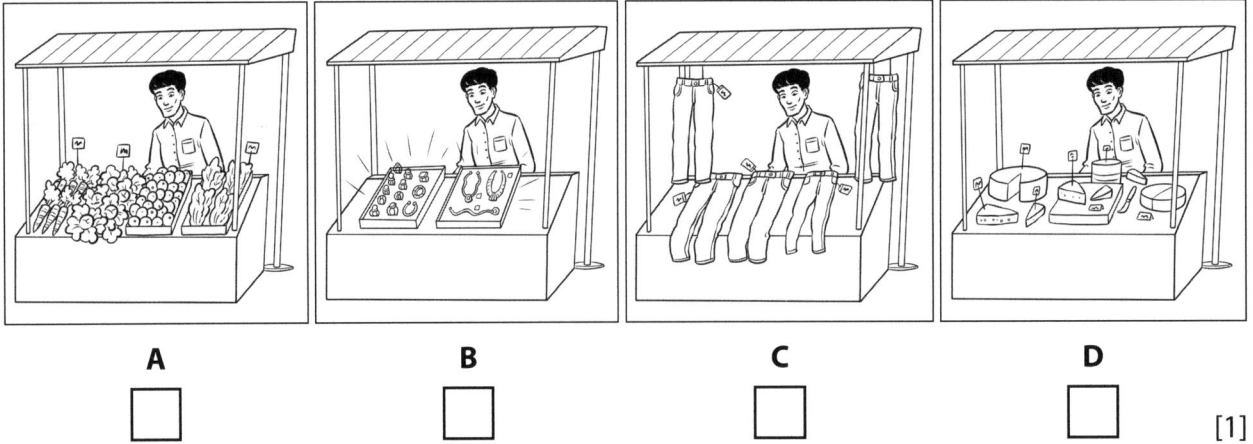

A ☐ B ☐ C ☐ D ☐ [1]

Question 6

What did the girl do with her cousin?

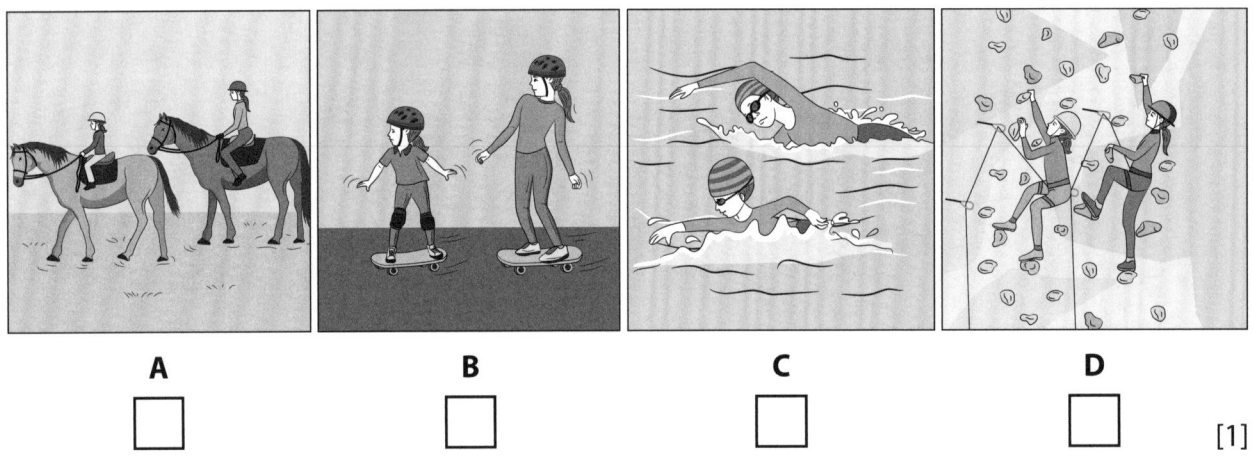

A ☐ B ☐ C ☐ D ☐ [1]

Audio for the listening exercises is available in the digital resource.

Question 7

What souvenir did the woman bring back from China?

A B C D [1]

Question 8

Why were the man's neighbours so noisy today?

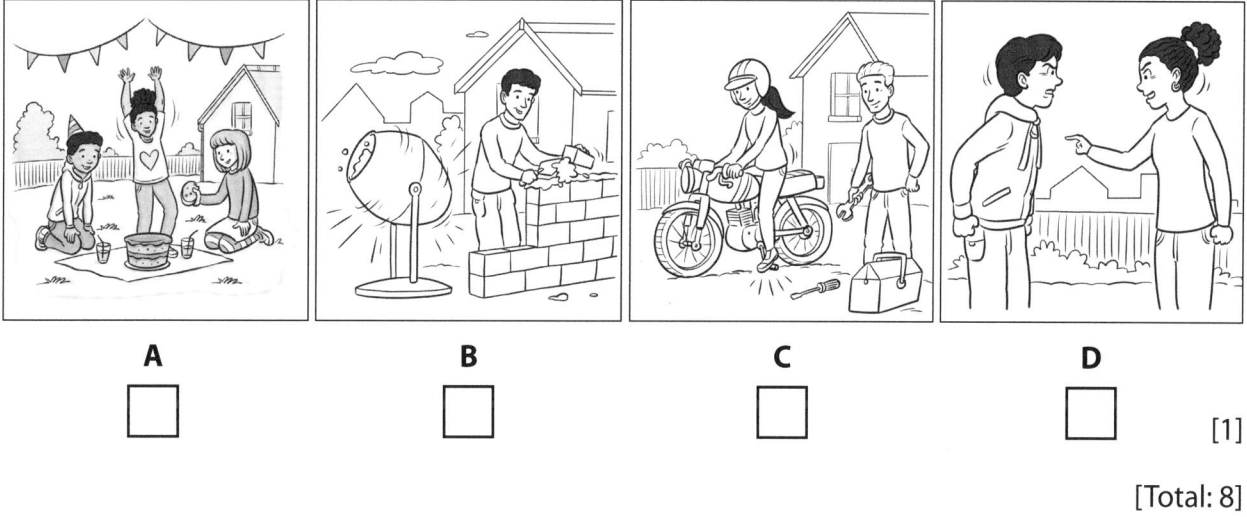

A B C D [1]

[Total: 8]

Audio for the listening exercises is available in the digital resource.

Exercise 2

 You will hear five short recordings. For each question, choose the correct answer **A**, **B** or **C**, and put a tick (✔) in the appropriate box.

You will hear each recording twice.

You will hear a boy talking about his interest in birds.

Question 9

Why did the boy take up birdwatching as a hobby?

A A relative persuaded him to try it.

B He was inspired by a TV programme.

C He did some research on birds for school.   [1]

Question 10

What has been the biggest problem so far?

A He does not live in the countryside.

B He cannot tell the difference between some birds.

C He does not have anyone his age to share his interest.   [1]

Audio for the listening exercises is available in the digital resource.

You will hear two friends talking about visiting an art gallery.

Question 11

What did the friends like about the gallery?

A the amount of space ☐

B the range of art ☐

C the helpful staff ☐ [1]

Question 12

What does the girl say about the sculptures?

A They looked surprisingly unattractive. ☐

B They were similar to things she had seen before. ☐

C They did not appear to be in the right place. ☐ [1]

You will hear a man talking about working with a fitness instructor.

Question 13

The man chose the fitness instructor because

A she was recommended by a friend. ☐

B she seemed to expect a lot from him. ☐

C she had a lot of qualifications. ☐ [1]

Question 14

What does the man feel about the sessions he has had so far?

A confused by some things he has being told ☐

B convinced the price he is paying is worth it ☐

C disappointed by the lack of progress he has made ☐ [1]

Audio for the listening exercises is available in the digital resource.

You will hear a woman leaving a voicemail message about her new job.

Question 15

Why did the woman change her job?

A She did not get on with her colleagues. ☐

B She wanted to have extra responsibility. ☐

C She found it too tiring. ☐   [1]

Question 16

What is an advantage of the woman's new job?

A She has developed a new skill. ☐

B She can take longer breaks. ☐

C She has opportunities to travel. ☐   [1]

You will hear a man talking about a meeting with family members.

Question 17

What does the man say about the meeting?

A It was a very emotional occasion. ☐

B It was similar to ones he had attended before. ☐

C It was badly organized. ☐   [1]

Question 18

The man was surprised when his grandfather told him about

A one relative's future plans. ☐

B something new about his family history. ☐

C an aspect of his father's character. ☐   [1]

[Total: 10]

Audio for the listening exercises is available in the digital resource.

Exercise 3

 You will hear a teacher called Mrs Collins giving a talk about the history of toys. For each question choose the correct answer, **A**, **B** or **C**, and put a tick (✔) in the appropriate box.

You will hear the talk twice.

Now look at questions **19–26**.

The history of toys

Question 19

Mrs Collins was surprised to find that … were created thousands of years ago.

A kites

B mechanical puzzles

C dolls [1]

Question 20

Mrs Collins says that she particularly likes an old toy made from

A bronze.

B clay.

C wood. [1]

Audio for the listening exercises is available in the digital resource.

Question 21

In the eighteenth century, toys such as … were given to children to improve their knowledge of the world.

A   board games

B   puppet theatres

C   toy soldiers   [1]

Question 22

Mrs Collins was impressed that in the nineteenth century, children could even use toy … when they played with their dolls' houses.

A   meat

B   furniture

C   medicine   [1]

Question 23

At the beginning of the 1900s, toys known as … were popular with children.

A   model trains

B   wooden blocks

C   construction sets   [1]

Audio for the listening exercises is available in the digital resource.

Question 24

Today more and more … are sold as toys to give publicity to television series or films.

A superheroes ☐

B action figures ☐

C cartoon characters ☐ [1]

Question 25

Mrs Collins was most impressed by the … that went on sale after Armstrong walked on the Moon.

A toy astronauts ☐

B moon creatures ☐

C space rockets ☐ [1]

Question 26

One of the earliest electronic games, known as … taught children a useful skill.

A Merlin ☐

B Auto Race ☐

C The Little Professor ☐ [1]

[Total: 8]

Audio for the listening exercises is available in the digital resource.

Exercise 4

 You will hear six people talking about their experiences of visiting famous tourist attractions.

For questions **27–32**, choose from the list (**A–H**) showing which idea each speaker expresses. Write the correct letter (**A–H**) on the answer line. Use each letter only once. There are two extra letters which you do not need to use.

You will hear the recordings twice.

Now read statements **A–H**.

| **A** | It took too long for me to see everything. |

| **B** | I experienced a range of different emotions. |

| **C** | It was difficult to get there. |

| **D** | It was very different from what I had expected. |

| **E** | It was so crowded that I could not enjoy being there. |

| **F** | It was very good value for money. |

| **G** | It had excellent facilities for visitors. |

| **H** | I am sure I will return there soon. |

Question 27	Speaker 1	[1]
Question 28	Speaker 2	[1]
Question 29	Speaker 3	[1]
Question 30	Speaker 4	[1]
Question 31	Speaker 5	[1]
Question 32	Speaker 6	[1]

[Total: 6]

Audio for the listening exercises is available in the digital resource.

Exercise 5

You will hear an interview with a man called Alex Murray, an actor who works in the theatre. For each question, choose the correct answer, **A**, **B** or **C**, and put a tick (✔) in the appropriate box.

You will hear the interview twice.

Now look at questions **33–40**.

Question 33

Alex says that being on stage is more enjoyable for him because

A it gives him a greater sense of achievement. ☐

B the pressure he feels makes him perform better. ☐

C he gets immediate feedback on how he is doing. ☐ [1]

Question 34

When Alex was given his first acting part in a school play,

A he was excited to be given such an opportunity. ☐

B nobody seemed to mind that he did not perform well. ☐

C it was because his friend had recommended him. ☐ [1]

Question 35

What is Alex's attitude to the auditions he attends?

A He gets annoyed by the way they are organised. ☐

B He accepts them as something he cannot avoid. ☐

C He is confident he can predict whether he will be successful. ☐ [1]

Question 36

How does Alex prepare when he gets a new part?

A He depends on his imagination to create the character. ☐

B He studies other actors who have had the same role. ☐

C He talks to other actors in the play about their roles. ☐ [1]

Audio for the listening exercises is available in the digital resource.

Question 37

What does Alex say about learning his lines?

A It is only possible if he works closely with others. ☐

B It is not something that causes many difficulties. ☐

C It is easier for him to do it at a particular time. ☐ [1]

Question 38

What does he say about working with directors?

A He is willing to accept most of their ideas. ☐

B He believes some can waste time discussing details. ☐

C He can find their different approaches confusing. ☐ [1]

Question 39

When Alex wears his costume for the first time,

A he thinks again about the character he's going to play. ☐

B he tends to ask for changes to be made. ☐

C he begins to feel nervous about the play. ☐ [1]

Question 40

How does Alex feel about the reviews of the plays he is in?

A He is aware that he can learn something from them. ☐

B He doubts that the journalists understand the theatre. ☐

C He is annoyed that they focus on the negative points. ☐ [1]

[Total: 8]

Audio for the listening exercises is available in the digital resource.

Examiner copy: Practice Test 4 – Speaking

Warm-up (1–2 minutes)

Put the student at ease by conducting a short conversation using the following questions:

- What do you normally do after school?
- Where did you go on your last holiday?
- How often do you watch films?

Part 1 – Interview (2–3 minutes)

Tell the student the topic for this part (time). Conduct a short interview with the student by asking the following questions. If the student does not know how to answer the question, ask the question again. If the student still does not know what to say, move on to the next question.

Time

- What are the situations in life when time is important, and why?
- Can you tell me about a situation when you didn't have enough time to do something, and what happened?
- When do you think young people should move out of their parents' house, and why?

Part 2 – Short talk (3–4 minutes including 1 minute preparation time)

Ask the student to look at their card, which contains the following speaking assessment information. The student has up to 1 minute to read the card and prepare for the talk. The student cannot make any written notes. After one minute, ask the student to start their short talk.

Voluntary work

You are planning to do some voluntary work during your school holidays. You are considering the following options:

- looking after animals on a farm
- helping older people in your local area.

Discuss the benefits and challenges of each option. Say which option you would prefer, and why.

Part 3 – Discussion (3–4 minutes)

Conduct a discussion using the following questions. If the student says very little, encourage a further discussion by asking questions like, *Why do you think so?, Can you tell me a bit more about …?*, etc. If the student does not know what to say, give them a few seconds, then move on to the next question.

- Some people say that all work, including voluntary work, should be paid. What do you think?
- Should voluntary work be compulsory for young people? What is your opinion?
- Do you think that being a farmer is one of the most important jobs? Why? Why not?
- There is an opinion that animal charities are not as important as charities which help people. Would you agree?

Student copy: Practice Test 4 – Speaking

IMPORTANT: Do not look at this card until the examiner tells you to.

Speaking assessment card

Voluntary work

You are planning to do some voluntary work during your school holidays. You are considering the following options:

- looking after animals on a farm
- helping older people in your local area.

Discuss the benefits and challenges of each option. Say which option you would prefer, and why.

BLANK PAGE

Acknowledgements

The authors and publishers acknowledge the following sources of copyright material and are grateful for the permissions granted. While every effort has been made, it has not always been possible to identify the sources of all the material used, or to trace all copyright holders. If any omissions are brought to our notice, we will be happy to include the appropriate acknowledgements on reprinting.

Thanks to Getty Images (GI) for permission to reproduce images:

Cover Andriy Onufriyenko/GI; **PT1 R&W E1** Westend61/GI; **PT1 L Q2** Alexander Spatari/GI; kate_sept2004/GI; Catherine Falls Commercial/GI; Travelpix Ltd/GI; **PT1 L Q4** Cokada/GI; Digital Vision/GI; South_agency/GI; **PT2 R&W E1** Krasyuk/iStock/GI; E5 Monkeybusinessimages/GI; **PT2 L Q1** FillipoBacci/GI; Caia Image/GI; Sorapong Chaipanya/GI; Cavan Images/GI; **PT2 L Q3** Westend61/GI; Paul Souders/GI; Cinoby/GI; Pierre-Yves Babelon/GI; **PT2 L Q6** Michael Kai/GI; Barry Winiker/GI; Martinedoucet/GI; Miodrag ignjatovic/GI; **PT2 L Q8** Rubberball/Mark Andersen/GI; Thepalmer/GI; Chuck Savage/GI; Uniquely India/GI; **PT2 L E3** Thomas Kitchin & Victoria Hurst/All Canada Photos/GI; **PT3 R&W E1** Mitchell Krog/GI; **PT3 R&W E3** Matthew Micah Wright/Lonely Planet Images/GI; **PT3 R&W E5** JohnnyGreig/GI; **PT3 L Q2** FatCamera/GI; John Lamb/GI; Miodrag Ignjatovic/GI; Xavierarnau/GI; **PT3 L Q4** Tim de Waele/GI; ANP/GI; **PT4 R&W E1** Daniel Garcia/AFP/GI; **PT4 R&W E3** Sergeyskleznev/GI; **PT4 R&W E5** Baranozdemir/GI; **PT4 L Q7** Grzegorz Wozniak/GI; RyanKing999/GI; Design56/GI; Floortje/GI